PRAISE FOR *SPIRIT RESCUE*

"This book is very much about the same spirit world I documented with Kerrie in *Suburban Psychic,* a very well-received program on ABC Radio National. Even if you're an agnostic like me, this book is full of interesting insights into a dimension that she sees vividly. Kerrie is working for the good side."

—Greg Appel, Australian documentary maker

"This book is such a gripping read. I could not put it down. It is so interesting and informative, especially the chapter on angels. I will call upon Archangel Michael and Raphael more often so I know I am protected. The information about the psychic imprint is so true. I am often buzzing with joy for days after a positive celebration like an engagement or wedding and never understood why. Now I do ... Everyone needs a copy of this book in their home."

—Jane Brady, managing director of PTV Australia

"A compelling digest of spiritual manifestations on the earth and etheric planes."

—Reverend Lynne Weston, Ramsgate Spiritual Church

SPIRIT

RESCUE

KERRIE ERWIN

SPIRIT

RESCUE

Clear Negative Energy
and Free Earthbound Souls

Llewellyn Publications
Woodbury, Minnesota

FIRST EDITION
First Printing, 2023

Book design by M. Brasington
Cover design by Kevin R. Brown
Editing by Marjorie Otto

Llewellyn Publications is a registered trademark of Llewellyn Worldwide Ltd.

Library of Congress Cataloging-in-Publication Data (Pending)
ISBN: 978-0-7387-7432-9

Llewellyn Publications
A Division of Llewellyn Worldwide Ltd.
2143 Wooddale Drive
Woodbury, MN 55125-2989
www.llewellyn.com

Printed in the United States of America

About the Author

Sydney-based medium Kerrie Erwin has lived between two worlds since childhood and is able to *see, sense,* and *hear* spirit people talking. Realizing her true calling when she was very young, she now works professionally as a spiritual medium and clairvoyant, working with spirit rescue, hauntings, and connecting people to loved ones that have passed over into the spirit world. She also teaches metaphysics, reads tarot cards, and works with feng shui. She is trained in spiritual hypnotherapies and past-life regression. She works via phone, Skype, and the media all over Australia and overseas, helping people with her abilities.

Closely aligned to her healing work is Kerrie's vibrant creative nature, as she regularly works in club shows, radio, and around the country. Kerrie has also written several books, has been featured on different radio shows as a guest speaker, and is a highly sought-after writer. She also has a column for the *Sydney Observer*, contributes to publications and magazines as a freelance writer, and has written many well publicized articles on the paranormal over the years.

Coming from a media background as a stage and film actor, she has also hosted her own show on cable TV for many years, called *Let's Have a Chat with Kerrie*. She's also worked as a guest on *Psychic TV,* starred in *All About You*, and worked on Sydney's Channel 7. Her aim as a spiritual medium is to help as many people as possible, to teach others that love is eternal, and to inspire others to believe in themselves. She currently has her own Facebook spirit show called the *Kerrie Erwin Spirit Show* to educate and help people.

As an author, her books to date are *Magical Tales of the Forest, Memoirs of a Suburban Medium*, and *Spirits Whispering in My Ear, Tarot for Light Workers, Sacred Soul, Sacred Space, Sacred Signs, Clearing* and *Mediumship*.

CONTENTS

INTRODUCTION

Death as we know it is a natural transition to the spirit world. The majority of spirits generally cross after death, but there are others that do not for a number of reasons. These spirits are called lost souls or earthbound spirits. They live in a different reality. They do not belong here in our dimension and are not pets for us to collect. These earthbound or lost souls live in the astral, are often confused and wander aimlessly around in a gray, cold murky existence, not understanding they are dead. The astral plane they live in is called an in-between world and is described as bleak, gray, with little or no warmth with often dark, murky spirits floating around everywhere. It is my job as a medium to do the rescue work so that these souls can move on to the spirit world where they receive healing, and then return to their own soul groups for healing and reincarnation.

I believe in ghosts: they are everywhere and sometimes they may appear human, like us mere mortals, yet again they can also be dark figures or silver shadows of the night that you see flash past from the corner of your eyes, making you feel confused and agitated.

In folklore, a ghost or ghoul is the soul or spirit of a dead person or animal that can appear in the living. Ghosts are often described as shimmers in the night, with an invisible, cold, translucent presence, and can often appear as tiny black cold dots all joined together that disappear when you touch them. Often, they will leave psychic imprints or energy, like spider webs, or residue, which is a type of energy you experience when confronted by a ghost to let us know they still exist. I have seen lifelike ghostly shadows of men, women, children, and animals, and some people will say they have seen this as well. Each experience that you have is different and always quite remarkable.

As a small child I saw visiting spirits all the time, like family members or people I once knew, after they died. I also saw spooky spirits or earthbound spirits that never wanted to go away, and unfortunately they would just hang around all the time, in my own home and my grandmother's. They were unpleasant, persistent, and extremely annoying. Sometimes I just felt as if they were following me all the time, to get my attention.

My grandmother was a widow who lived alone in a historical older part of Sydney that was renowned for being very shady in its shipping days and a tough working area. The old terrace she lived in was what I can only describe as a very old creepy house that smelled peculiar and always had strange things going on of a paranormal nature. It had its own history of human tragedy, over the years, as there was not only a death in the family, but a tragic suicide. The old three-story terrace home was not only miserable and unloved, but haunting, as it was full of so many sad memories, negative energy, and lots of ghosts. It was three levels, joined together by an old staircase that led up to an unused attic at the top with holes in the floorboards. All the rooms were always locked, dusty, and dangerous dad said, as nobody ever used the rooms on the top floors as they were all falling to pieces from years and years of neglect. Being a curious child and wanting to discover and explore everything around me, this made me more determined to find out what was inside those mysterious rooms. As I was used to seeing spirits from as long as I could remember, I have never, in my whole life seen such a large collection of annoying spirits in one place, just walking around the place and going about their business as if they did not have a care in the world.

From my experience over the years with spirit rescue, there are always a few lost spirits lurking around, not only one, as they like to integrate with other spirits, but often living or hiding in different sections of the home or space.

One of the lost spirits was a very elderly spirit woman, that always sat on an old rocking chair on the front veranda, as you entered the home. She reminded me of a guard dog as she was terrifying to look at. The spirit woman was always there each time we arrived. On appearance, she had long, thin white hair that she wore tied back in a small bun at the back of her head. Often when my parents and I arrived at the house in our tiny car for our weekly visits, she would always just stare straight ahead, as if she was looking at something in the distance. Nobody else could see her except me. No matter how many times I whinged, cried,, and complained, refusing to get out of the car, I was always ignored. Before too long, I just gave up and learned to say nothing as it was a waste of time and not worth the effort, unless I wanted the wrath of my mother as she would get really furious. The trouble was nobody else in the family could see spirits, or believe in them for that matter, and I was told constantly not to make up silly stories and told it was just my incredible imagination.

As for the spirit woman, I had no interest in anything to do with her, so over time we had a type of standoff and pretended not to see each other, as it was better that way. Whenever I tried to take a sneaky look at her, she would instantly disappear into thin air, as if it was some type of stupid game. Determined to know who she was, I found out later while exploring the house that the old woman spirit lived in one of Nanna's locked rooms upstairs. My curiosity got the better of me one day when I could hear muffled sounds coming from one of the rooms upstairs while playing with my sister on the stairs. Thinking it was time to find out what was going on, I decided to investigate it myself, making my younger sister my lookout. It was safe to do as the adults would never know. They were all too busy in Nanna's small kitchen at the back of the house drinking endless cups of tea and eating my mother's fruit cakes. I could not believe my eyes when I sneaked up the old stairs and peeked through a keyhole of one of the locked doors. The muffled sounds I soon discovered were coming from inside, but I could never figure out or hear what they were saying. Somehow the spirits must have known I was there, because as I peered through the keyhole and then pressed my ear against the wooden door to try and hear, the noise suddenly stopped and there was nothing but a deathly silence. One day I stopped going up the stairs—I got the shock of my life when I saw a huge black eye looking through the keyhole back at me. Screaming in fear, I dove down the stairs as quickly as I could go and landed on my sister's head.

Over the years, as a child I also witnessed and saw other spirit people that came from other houses on the street as well. They were all different shapes and sizes, and they used to just walk

From my own experience, the reason lost souls are here is that of leaving unfinished business here on earth: it may be an unknown fear or having some type of attachment in the living world. To survive on our plane, they are attracted to and need our life force, energy, light, and warmth. They need people for this and that's why you will never find an earth spirit in a lonely place as they feed off our energy. If allowed to stay on our earthy plane, people that have an earthbound spirit will get sick over time because, like vampires of the night, these spirits will suck our energy and create trails of havoc, depleting us of energy, which in turn will upset the natural *chi* and balance of our world. Most of these earthbound spirits are harmless and probably more scared of you, but there are a few that cause havoc and can be very negative, causing harm to people in the spaces they choose to invade and linger in. As for demonic beings, which are evil, I have not had a lot of experience as I choose not to work with that particular energy, but when I am called I will always offer assistance and use extra protection. I have experienced very dark, sickly, negative energy, especially around murder scenes or where terrible atrocities have occurred, so that's why I pulled away from that energy. I once had to help a friend, an empath who was doing paid work for a charity that worked in a red-light district of a city that was full of drugs, criminals, and shady people. After working the night shift for a couple of weeks, he complained of a heavy dark octopus-type of energy that had somehow wrapped itself around his hands and neck. Terrified, he rang for assistance because no matter how hard he tried to remove the horrible thing, with smoke cleansing and spiritual healing, he found it wouldn't budge. When I asked him what it felt like, he described it as being threatening, dark, cold, and sticky. He also said it had some type of intelligence and that it was quite malevolent. Hearing the fear in his voice, I decided to help him straight away. The next day I drove over to his house, and after a few attempts we finally got rid of the horrible thing together. Afterward, I gave him a spiritual healing and made sure I put extra light in his aura. I also advised him to have an Epsom salt bath to ground and clear his energy field as the whole thing was exhausting and had really knocked him around. Grateful, he thanked me, but said it really shook his confidence.

There was a period when I worked with missing people and murder cases in a group for the police, but the dark lingering energy that hung around from that work was unbearable. It seemed to affect everyone in my household as the negative energy lingered around constantly and my husband did not want me to be involved as it was too upsetting for him. He kept saying I was bringing it home to our household. I tired of the constant arguments and him peering out of the windows every time he heard a noise. He kept saying he was convinced that the criminals would follow me home and we would all get murdered. I soon left the group. In hindsight, I also found murdered victims were hard to talk to, as they were still traumatized and needed healing. As a working medium, you get to know your strengths and that was not mine, especially when working on so many gruesome cases with innocent victims and children.

Today almost everyone has had some type of encounter or experience with a ghost, whether it's a ghost tour, spooky stories from friends, work colleagues, loved ones, or generally just people encountered in everyday life. In fact, as soon as I mention what I do, people will always tell me about some kind of encounter, as if they can finally tell someone. These days there is confirmation of the existence of ghosts through television shows about experienced paranormal investigators and haunted places, from reports on social media—some more gruesome than the next. The work I do is called *spirit rescue* and this involves me sending spirits back into the spirit world. I have met many different types of people from all walks of life and nationalities that have experienced this type of phenomenon. It's hard to believe the number of cases mediums like myself have worked on and the stories we could tell.

Take the Tower of London for example: to an empath, such as me, it is a torturous and evil place, and the sheer horror of its existence still lingers on to this day. Its trails of residual energy and horrific psychic negative energy has sunk deep from history into the buildings and implanted its cellular memories of torture, cruelty, and grief into the surrounding walls.

Gruesome hauntings from terrible and unthinkable atrocities in history have been left like filthy and morbid stains everywhere, showing the fragility of the human error. My experience as I have described was not by any means a good one, or enjoyable for that matter. In fact, memories of that place when I visited many years ago affected me energetically for a long time. Looking back, I had not been at the Tower for very long when I found I had to leave, as I felt very sick and could not stop burping loudly. I remember holding vomit in the back of my mouth. Psychically, I could hear the pain of spirits calling out: agonizing screaming in my ears which really affected me as an empath. It took me quite a while to recover from the dreadful experience and it is a place I would never visit again.

Historically, I am sure there are many places like that in the world. I have to say we as mediums must be more mindful of closing down and wearing protection next time we decide to visit such a toxic place, as not to feel affected. Not everyone on the planet is love and light. Humans, as we know from our history, are often caught up in their ego, religion, or ridiculous beliefs. We can be very cruel and take great pleasure to incite violence. Some people often lack compassion for others. As for the dark souls that caused so much carnage on our planet, let them receive their karma for the injustices they leave behind.

From an early age, I knew my purpose was to help people with my mediumship and psychic gifts. After studying mediumship in spiritual churches, sitting in development circles for years with trance mediumship, and running my own closed group with seances, I gradually developed very strong guides to join my spirit team of highly evolved angel helpers. It was no surprise, I was later told by my guide White Feather and one of my old teachers from my early days as a young medium, that I would be doing rescue work. Spirit rescue is, by far, one of the rarest forms of mediumship, as there are not a lot of people that can actually do the work. Spirit rescue guides can create a strong link the to the lost entity for clear communication to help them cross into the light, through a vortex of light into the spirit world, which is another dimension. As a mental medium, mainly working with voice and clairvoyance, I see and hear the spirits talking. I also work with trance and psychical mediumship as part of my practice because it gives me a better perspective when being of service and offering all my gifts. Over the years, I have worked hands-on with all kinds of sprites and spirits, living and lost—seeing, sensing and talking to them from as far back as I can remember.

Sending these often lost and confused souls healing, compassion, and love.

Keep the faith.

Kerrie

CHAPTER 1

WHAT IS SPIRIT RESCUE?

Spirit rescue is known, in Spiritualism, as the practice of assisting lost souls or spirit entities who are believed to have failed to make the transition into the afterlife. It can be done by non-Spiritualists with dedicated training and practice with a good teacher, just like I experienced in my early training at a Spiritualist church years ago. We call this *rescue work* or helping lost spirits cross over. It is important to understand that lost souls, or earthbound spirits, do not belong here and are certainly not for our amusement, as some people may think. They are stuck in an in-between world, which is not a pleasant place as there is no love, light, or any chance to reach the spirit world where they receive healing and reincarnate once again and return to earth for lessons and learning.

Earthbound, lost souls, and different types of entities do exist in our world; it is not just the senses playing up or your incredible imagination. Over time, it is mentally and psychically impossible to ignore the paranormal activity going on in your surroundings because these lost souls drain your energy and cause havoc in your world.

Once you have realized that your psychic senses are real and things do not feel right in your space, home, or energy field, it is time to act. Lost souls create havoc to your space and upset the natural chi of our world, creating imbalance, and need to be cleared.

The reason I do this work is because I am inundated by so many people who have problems with hauntings. I don't go looking for them, they come to me wanting help. Most are terrified, do not understand what is going on, and need my help. Often, they will say how relieved they are to find me because unless you have had this experience, it is hard to believe this type of thing exists. People are very quick to condemn the use of psychics even though, in reality, we are a valuable asset to humanity because we are here for service.

As a medium, spirit rescue is a simple job: all I have to do is tune in to the energy, locate the lost soul, and call on my amazing spirit team that usually do all the work by giving the lost spirit assistance to cross. Once the procedure is over, the lost soul does not come back. If someone would have told me that this was going to be a large part of my life's work as a spiritual medium, I never would have believed them: crawling under houses, going into old basements, and digging around in attics, all to find these lost souls, is not pleasant, to say the least. Years later when I started to work remotely, it was much easier and faster with all the work I had to do. Now, I don't get dirty, see spiders, see rats, or see anything scary. I cannot believe how effective remote rescue really is and I am amazed at how easy it is to do.

Why I Started Rescuing Spirits

If it hadn't been for the annoying ghost in my parents' house that kept me up all night when I was a small child growing up, I would not have bothered to pursue my work as a medium and spirit rescuer. I soon discovered these spirits were everywhere and not just in my family's home. It is not the type of work that is glamorous, nor is it for the fainthearted.

Every single night, like clockwork, just when I was about to fall asleep, I would always hear the same heavy footsteps coming from outside my bedroom from the laundry that would wake me up. Once the noise stopped, I would awake suddenly and as I peered from under the cotton sheets, I would see a tall spirit man dressed in a suit, standing right next to my bed, silently staring down at me. Not knowing what to do, one night I reached out to try and touch him but my hand went right through his body, which was made up of little black and gray dots that were ice cold. Terrified, I shivered in fear and dove under the sheet until he went away. Every time I heard the same footsteps, I shuddered with fear until he left. Sometimes I would feel paralyzed, and, to my horror, the ghastly monster, if I tried to ignore him, would jump on my head as if trying to strangle me, making it impossible to breathe. He would also lie on top of me so I could not breathe.

These nights were terrifying for a young child. Too scared to sleep in my own bed and my mother having had enough, she said I could leave the bathroom light on, which acted as a deterrent because everything seemed to stop after that. I still to this day have a night light on, as I find it impossible to sleep in a very dark room.

The weird thing was even though I hadn't seen that particular ghost for years, I got the shock of my life when I accidentally discovered where he lived one day. While washing my hands in my parents' laundry room, I began to feel my hairs sticking up and goose bumps all over my body for no apparent reason. Not understanding what was going on, I suddenly had the most sickening feeling that something, or someone, was watching me from above my head. Slowly looking up, I saw an eye watching me through a crack in the manhole in the ceiling. Horrified, I felt sick in my stomach and started to burp, like I wanted to vomit, as I could just sense the thing sizing me up menacingly.

Lost Souls are Earthbound

After that experience I rang the minister from the Spiritualist church, who was also my first teacher, to tell her what had happened in my parent's laundry room. Thinking it amusing, she just laughed and said, "It was just a lost soul, a spirit that is earthbound. They can't hurt you, love, as it's probably more scared of you, so don't worry, dear." Not really understanding what she was talking about, I asked her to explain.

"Lost souls are earthbound, or stuck," she said. "They have not crossed when they have died for certain reasons, don't really understand they are dead, and they live between two worlds, wandering around, confused, lonely, and fearful. They are very different to the spirits you connect with in the church, which are connected to our love eternally," she explained. She then went on to say, "You need to help it cross by telling the lost spirit it is dead, does not belong here, and it needs to go. Tell it to open its eyes and look into the light. That's why it's been pestering you all these years; it needs your help. Once you've done this, your own spirit team will step in and heavenly help will be on its way, as spirit will always look after its own. The lost soul will be pulled slowly into the dimension called the spirit world like a large tracking beam."

She also kindly explained the reason it kept coming to me, night after night, standing at the end of my bed in silence. It was trying to get my attention because it could see my natural light of being a medium and knew I could help it. Finally, she nearly made me faint when she said, "And don't be surprised because one day you will have many cases like this. There are no accidents in the spirit world you know," she laughed. "This is all part of your spiritual contract. You have a big team of guides that are here to assist you to do the work, so you are not alone. Yes dear, you have plenty of assistance, so don't go worrying because your own spirit team has come here to earth to help you with your life's work."

Without further comment, she hung the phone up and left me feeling sick at the other end. I look back at those early days and remember it took a lot of courage to go back and do it, but once I did and finally saw it disappear, it never came back again, and I never again felt any fear. These days I just go with the flow, and I have continued to do the work, year after year, exactly like she said without any problems whatsoever.

I will always be very grateful to this kind and amazing woman, as she was my first teacher in those early days. She was a great inspiration to me and appeared at the right time in my life because no one else I knew had any idea what I was on about. She also taught me to believe in myself and my abilities. She continues to have a profound influence on me to this day.

I believe that everybody on the planet has some type of spiritual gift, you just have to find out what it is, as we are all different. If you want to develop these gifts, it is just a matter of believing in yourself and spending time learning to meditate to still your mind and finding a good teacher. Your ability to tap into things will give you much insight to your inner world and the world around us. The more time you take to work on yourself will help you release negative patterns and karma by connecting and working with your higher self. Meditation also helps you become more aware of the people around you and teaches you everything there is to know about the gift and beauty of the Great Spirit.

Throughout my years as a spirit rescuer, I don't know how many times I have arrived at a place, only to be told by the client I was the sixth person to clear the space and the client wondering if I could get results. I have also heard that there is no such thing as a lost soul, only visiting souls, but through my many years of rescue work and experience I can honestly say there are numerous lost souls on the planet that need this valuable work.

Over time, I eventually became too busy to physically clear spirits in person and now have many cases overseas as well. That's why it is so good I can work over the phone remotely and get good results.

My work with the rescue includes spirit attachment removal, rescue techniques, closing vortexes, portals, clearing residual energy, and releasing negative energy. Any time I have difficulty or get a sense that the work will require more people, I will always bring somebody else in to help, such as a dowser or energy worker, because if the job is difficult and too big, it takes a lot of energy to work solo. It can be exhausting to free stubborn lost souls separated from the light and that are stuck while living in the astral plane.

I truly believe with more education and awareness, people will be able to learn how to rid themselves of spirits to a degree, but it is always advisable to call a professional in if warranted and the problem still exists.

What Happens with Spirit Rescue

We live in an incredible world and many of us are becoming more and more aware of the spiritual world around us. We are waking up to new realities. Once we understand we are not alone and are connected to so many spiritual helpers, angels, and loved ones in the spirit world, we realize that love is the most powerful energy in the world. Love is eternal and lives on. My message to everyone is seek help if need be. You no longer must live in darkness. There is always someone ready to step in and give assistance, no matter how hard it may seem.

"Look, I know this sounds crazy and I don't know what to do. I saw your card in a shop last week and for some reason I picked it up. I was visiting my father at the graveyard a few weeks ago and I kept feeling a strong presence of a male spirit when I got home. While I was watching TV, I kept feeling a strong invisible force pressing down on me. I tried to ignore it, thinking I was tired, but every time I got off my chair and walked into the kitchen, I could smell strong cigarette smoke and I felt totally nauseous. Also, I could not sleep last night as I kept hearing things being moved around. When I jumped up and put the light on it all stopped suddenly, but as soon as I got back into bed the noises continued into the early hours of the morning. Can you please help?"

My Response as a Medium

"Sure, I understand. You are not mad. I do this work a lot, so I believe you. Please put me on loudspeaker and walk to the front entrance of the home. Don't worry, you will be fine. The spirit is just trying to get your attention. Once you have done this, slowly walk through each room, telling me where you are. When I have detected a spirit, I will let you know."

As we entered her lounge room, I detected a spirit standing by the window in the far left corner. Burping loudly, as the energy always hits me in my solar plexus, I said loudly over the phone, "Go into the light. You are dead. Go, you do not belong here. Go now. Open your eyes and go. Your loved ones are waiting for you on the other side. Go now. Your time is finished. Go now."

Once I have said this a couple of times, I will feel an energy shift and I yawn. This indicates to me the spirit has left. The client will always say they felt a shiver, have goose bumps, or had a weird sensation when the spirit has crossed.

Even though we felt that energy shift, I will still instruct my client to keep walking room by room—inside cupboards, under beds, toilets, roof, anywhere a spirit can hide. After I have finished, I generally give the client a reading, especially if loved ones are around them in spirit, as generally there are many messages. I then assure them everything will be okay.

An Experience of Spirit Rescue in My Own Home

I have had many spirit rescues in the different homes I've lived in, but the worst was when I was badly injured. I still, to this day, have pain and a scar on my lower left leg from my battle. This memorable spirit rescue experience was a painful one for me. The sharp, crippling anguish from my smashed leg sent unbelievable waves of sheer, agonizing pain throughout my whole body, like burning wildfire, making me shake and scream in agony. Angry and overcome with shock, I watched helplessly while lying on the bathroom floor, a sinister looking black thing, like a menacing shadow, flash past over me, then suddenly disappeared out through the light tiles of the nearly renovated bathroom wall. Stunned, I could not believe what had just happened, but determined not to let the spirit get the better of me, I crawled my way to the door for help so I could process the damage and work out if I had broken my leg which was now the size of a swollen and red watermelon. My sensible brain from my old nursing days kicked in, like it was on automatic pilot and it kept telling me to move quickly and elevate my leg for minimal damage. *You'll be okay; don't worry, you have this,* kept repeating in my brain but the damage to my leg didn't look too good. My initial concern grew into anxiety and then to despair. In hindsight, I had no idea I was in any type of trouble and could not in a million years believe I was just about to have a careless accident. Only minutes ago, I had been lying luxuriously in the warm soapy bath, full to the rim with bubbles, unaware anything terrible was about to happen. The crazy thing was I was actually getting psychic warning signs for a while, as I had felt myself being watched, with prying invisible eyes from an unknown source directly from the back of my head. Refusing to give it any energy, I decided to just ignore it and hoped it would just go away while I continued to chat to my friend on the phone about a spirit show at a venue we were booked to do the next night.

It was a new venue, so we were excited to give it a go, as they had sold a lot of tickets and had people interested in coming. Instead of telling the unwanted spirit to leave and go into the light, or wherever it came from, I just ignored it, thinking it could wait and I would deal with it later, even though I was feeling sick in the stomach and gently burping for quite a while. Whenever this happens, it is warning that an unwanted spirit is present or toxic energy is around, as my solar plexus goes into overdrive, like a psychic horn, or hidden radar, letting me know it is time to protect and defend myself.

Unfortunately, I should have listened to my gut and done something because the longer it was there, it became obviously more determined to remain, waiting to make its move and make a strike to get my attention. This type of thing has happened to me before in places like hotels or staying overnight for work conventions. This is because a large number of people stay in hotels, guest houses and convention or conference venues.

By the time I had arrived at the club the next night, I kept wondering how I was going to work or even how I was even going to walk, for that matter. I should not have worried because when the promoter told the club what had happened, they kindly organized a wheelchair for me. Before I had time to think, I was being whisked off to the room with the big stage where the audience was waiting patiently. I should not have worried because as soon as I was wheeled onto the stage and I was introduced, I could feel the spirit energy kicking in, like a huge thunderbolt, with energy like a thousand bolts of electrical current going through the top of my head, making all my hairs stand on edge.

When it was time to work, I jumped off the chair, connecting fully to the spirit energy and was walking and even running all over the stage because these sorts of things are common in my world. Spirit will never let an opportunity go by in order to get their messages of love across to loved ones in the audience. It was one of those incredible moments, this remarkable phenomenon which made me think without a doubt this was exactly what I was supposed to be doing with my work. I even went as far as to do a little dance, as if not believing what was happening myself, as the incredible waves of light and spirit energy soared throughout my whole body in pulsating waves. It was an incredible night of so many wonderful messages. The reality was that no sooner had I delivered the last message and began to close all my chakras, than the spirit energy slowly left from where it had come from and moved out of me, leaving me hobbling again, like an invalid, and back into the wheelchair again.

I have so many stories about this type of phenomena, like a tour I did years ago. No sooner had I arrived when I was suddenly hit with a severe case of bronchitis and could not stop coughing. Worried, I looked around and saw other mediums waiting to go on staring at me as if I were mad, frowning and talking among themselves. In my heart, I knew I would be okay, because spirit always looks after you and, in my head, I could hear my guide White Feather telling me not to worry.

Imagine my relief when one of the women, a very kind soul, came up, grabbed my hand and smiling very sweetly with a twinkle in her eye, told me not to worry as the spirit energy would kick in and the cough would go away. She was right, of course, and I still look back at that day in awe and believe it was spirit intervention giving me a helping hand.

As for the lost spirit in my home, I hunted it down and found the awful thing hiding in a cupboard. As soon as I found it, by scanning every nook and cranny in my home, I quickly crossed it over, told the confused spirit it was dead, did not belong here, to open its eyes and look into the light as it was time to go as it was in the wrong reality. The moment I said this, it suddenly vanished. I could then feel a lightness in the room and energy settling all around me. In the future, I will just be more careful and check the car next time when I go to venues for invisible and unwelcomed guests that might try and hitch a ride…

CHAPTER 2

LIVING SPIRITS AND EARTHBOUND SOULS

After our physical life on earth, our physical bodies die and our soul leaves the body to transition into spirit, generally very quickly. Once it has done this, the soul then crosses over into the light, accompanied by a loved one and a guardian angel. It is a good thing to know we are never alone when we die; we are always accompanied by our own guardian angel we are born with. In fact, through my years of work, I will often hear a spirit say they were helped by a loved one in spirit waiting for them as they return to their soul group. This is the case with children, animals, and those who passed in tragic deaths or murder. No one is forgotten and everyone is forgiven once they have crossed, no matter what type of life they have lived on earth. Once we cross, we return home, back into the spirit world. These living spirits are the spirits we connect to via mediumship and are connected to our love, which is eternal. All professional trained mediums have proved time and time again through survival evidence that our dearly departed loved ones are quite often around us and know what is going on in our current lives. They are never forgotten and always there to give us information or evidence to help in any way they can, showing us there is no death—just a transition to another world.

Earthbound spirits, on the other hand, do not cross after their transition toward the light for several reasons. From what I have experienced in my practice, earthbound spirits do not have the consciousness or intelligence to understand they are actually dead and are generally in a confused state, or type of limbo, which causes them to feel agitated, fearful, and stuck. As one could imagine, this astral state is cold, gray, and lonely. In order to stay here on earth, these spirits will intentionally live off our own energy, our life force, or *prana*, affecting our own health if left for long periods of time. This will always cause issues for everyone living in the affected area including pets, sometimes causing them to get sick, and, in some cases, die. It's amazing how animals can sense negative energies in a space and they will always let you know by refusing to go into the room, as if they are psychic. With earthbound spirits living in your home or work space, there will always be constant worries, a feeling of a dark cloud constantly in your life, and negativity that will linger the longer the lost spirit is there. Some of the reasons for this type of phenomenon are described in cases I have listed on the following pages, but sometimes it is not understood why.

Accidental Death, Long Illness, Fatal Accident, or Sudden Death

Often, the cases I have worked on the spirit in question does not understand they have died and for some reason stay here and have no intention of leaving. A woman rang me once and said she kept seeing a spirit woman hanging around her bedroom and quite often found pills on the floor that did not belong to her. She told me she felt sorry for her but was annoyed by all the noise at night. This was the worst thing that could have happened, as the spirit woman now wanted to stay and keep pestering my client.

I have also helped many lost spirits wandering around the places where they have been killed, such as road accidents. I once cleared a home where a woman who died in hospital decided to go home with her husband in his car and straight back to her bed. When I connected to her in spirit, she said she had no intention of going anywhere and wanted to stay in her home. She had been sick for many years with a mental health struggle and liked being looked after by her husband. She was upset about another woman in the home, whom her husband had met after the wife's death. The only way to persuade her to leave was by both of us telling her she was dead and that she needed to go. We reassured her that it was safe, and she no longer needed to stay in her sick body that was ravaged with disease. Once we did this several times, she took off very quickly and seemed happy to do so. Things soon went back to normal, and her husband's clothes and money stopped disappearing. As for the husband, he was happy to know she was finally gone and felt comforted in the fact that they both could move on with their own journeys.

Another case was of a young boy who tragically fell off a cliff and died. He was furious with himself, even though it was an accident. Instead of crossing over, he went back to his girlfriend's place and scared the living daylights out of her. Not knowing what to do, she finally contacted me, and we encouraged him to cross. All was forgiven and I told him he would have his time again one day through reincarnation when it was his chosen time to come back again.

Suicide

Some believe that people who commit suicide remain stuck or are not able to reach the spirit world. This is not true, as there is no judgment in the spirit world, and they generally cross safely like most souls. I have only seen a very few cases that have remained earthbound. People who believe that you end up in hell when you take your own life are simply speculating. If a soul dies a traumatic death, they generally come out of their earthly body before impact and are helped by their guides and the angelic realm to cross over safely into the spirit world. This goes for terrible accidents and murders as well. I worked on a murder case with a young girl once and she told me she left her body before the actual murder, which was a relief, and I was happy to share this with the client. I have also been told this by other spirits I have spoken to during readings. Many say they never suffered, such as a young woman who jumped off a cliff or a young man who stepped in front of a train because he was so depressed.

Once the spirit has crossed, they may end up in a holding space, a type of healing space of pure unconditional love, which I call the "place of oneness." Other names include the "spirit hospital" or the "healing sanctuary." My spirit guides have shown me this in dreams and meditations. I also experienced this space firsthand when I had my own near-death experience (NDE) in my early twenties while traveling overseas. I have witnessed this space many times with my work, and I love to tell everyone this important information as I believe it is good to know. As for suicides, most spirits cross over. They are not punished or thought upon of committing a "holy sin" that some people like to preach. There is no judgment in the spirit world. We are all equal, but the higher vibration you have, the more advanced soul group you will go to.

During the COVID-19 pandemic in 2020, I was receiving a large amount of suicide cases from families and friends for young people that had taken their lives through hanging, drug overdoses, and jumping off cliffs and bridges. As one could imagine, I was completely overwhelmed. The numbers were astronomically high and it was terrible to see that a lot of young anxious people were not coping at all because of all the turmoil and thinking that the world did not have a good future for them. Once I connected to all of them (except for a young boy who hanged himself and was difficult to connect to), they all seemed happy and content on the other side. They described how lovely it was over there but how sorry they were they had hurt their loved ones who were grieving from the terrible tragedy and trying to piece their lives together.

As for the boy, who from the poor connection I realized was earthbound and was living in the astral plane, I called out his name and when he appeared in my office, confused, I told him it was time to go and he needed to cross over into the light as there were loved ones on the other side waiting for him. Saying goodbye, I held hands with his mother, and we felt him gently leave, without him saying a thing. When the whole thing was over, we looked at each other with tears in our eyes. As one can imagine, the whole experience was very moving and something I will not forget for a very long while. I am sure his own spirit or ancestral guide would have finally caught up with him and taken him over and I believe it was only a matter of time, as the boy was very agitated and was in great need of spiritual healing.

I also had a woman who came to me who said she could feel her ex in her house and even felt his spirit crawl into bed with her. He had shot himself a few months before and, instead of crossing, she was convinced he had returned to her home. Horrified, she had yelled at him many times to go but nothing happened. Over time, his toxic earthbound energy made her sick, tired, and depressed. When I spoke to him, he seemed to know what was going on and kept repeating he was sorry, he did not want to go, and he told me to tell her how much he loved her. He said he killed himself because he had too many problems with drugs and could not get his life together. After we sent him off, all the negative heavy energy, which was so thick you could cut it with a bread knife, seemed to suddenly lift and disappear swiftly out the windows. In its place, a new cleaner energy enveloped the home and there were no more heavy footsteps, cigarette smells, nor gunshot smells and sounds. She was finally able to move on with her life and was so grateful I helped her.

Fear, Religious Beliefs, False Concepts

Fear is an illogical feeling and is caused by not knowing certain information. I have only had a few cases where I have talked to a lost spirit and had them tell me they were afraid to cross as they did not believe in God, thought there wasn't a heaven, and as far as they were concerned there was nothing out there, except a dark void and emptiness.

I once had a client whose father's spirit would not cross. He told me his father had molested him when he was young and that his father was a known and convicted sex offender. When the old man, whom he had not seen in years, died in jail, his spirit kept hanging around his son's (my client's) home and would not leave. His son was convinced the unwelcomed spirit was around because of his constant nightmares returning and the sickly scent of his father's aftershave that lingered in his apartment. Desperate for help, his partner rang me and asked for help. Once I connected to the earthbound spirit, the spirit told me he was too scared to cross as his belief was that he might end up in hell and God would punish him for his deeds on earth. When I told the spirit in a matter-of-fact manner that there was no such place, he went away quicky without bothering to say anything further or ask for forgiveness.

An Obsessive Love or Greed

I once had a case involving a woman who was complaining she could still feel her ex-lover in her home after he died under mysterious circumstances. He had been involved with some bad types and she had read one day in the paper that his body had been found in a suitcase. She felt his spirit around her all the time, which felt very bad and negative. After putting up with endless, sleepless nights of somebody ringing the doorbell, loud rapping on her bedroom wall, and her bed shaking by itself, a terrible realization occurred to her: it was probably him, wanting her attention because he never had a chance to say goodbye. Once I connected to the spirit in question, he spoke of some money he had hidden in a wall of their house in case she might need it. Once I gave her the message, all the disruption stopped. The spirit in question disappeared and never returned again. I never heard from her again after that, so I am positive the energy was cleared and the spirit in question got what he wanted, allowing him to finally move into the spirit world. As for the money, we never spoke of that, but I am happy she was looked after.

Another client was a young man who fell off a roof in anger after a terrible argument with his father. It was many years ago and I was still a student. The spirit came to me after banging on the walls and throwing chairs around the Spiritualist church hall where we were all working in as practising mediums. Everybody freaked out, including the teacher. We all screamed but I could very clearly hear a boy calling out, saying he wanted to connect to his father as they had unfinished business. He was also furious he had died, as he was not ready to go and told me this several times. Not knowing what to do, I told the teacher this and she just stared at me and said, "Well, tell him to stop now and if his father rings us I will give him your number." Doing what she said, I yelled out and told him to stop and everything went dead quiet. Feeling terrible, I went home that night and kept wondering why nobody else could hear him until I remembered what my old teacher said to me years ago when I was a young teenager: "We would all have different roles in our mediumship and work in different ways, depending on our gifts and the spiritual guides that worked with us."

About a week later, I got the call and was told I was to do a reading for the man who lost his son. He had, like the teacher said, been guided by the spirit to contact the Spiritualist church. Not feeling confident and freaking out (I had never read for anyone like this before), I rang up the teacher and said I couldn't do it. My teacher told me in a stern voice to relax and get myself together and that the boy in question was standing patiently next to me, waiting for his father. She was right of course. Everything went well, the boy told his father what he wanted, that he was sorry and was now ready to go. Wishing him all the best, the father and I told him to cross over and saying his last goodbye, he suddenly left. No sooner had he crossed than an incredible light lit up the room and the father and I stared at each other in utter awe.

The Spirit Doesn't Understand They Are Dead

I have come across many confused, lost souls in homes, streets, and busy places, just wandering around like lost sheep, with no idea they are dead. My senses have always told me they are just confused and not to be afraid as they are the ones with fear and not me. This knowledge always makes my job a lot easier. I remember I did a clearing of an estate that had constant problems and delays when the new people wanted to renovate. No matter what the new owners did there were always delays and problems with the local council, workers not turning up for the job, electricity and plumbing malfunctioning, everything possible going wrong. It was a total nightmare for the owners who had no idea what was going on and were at each other's throats, as I can only imagine all the money they were spending and the frustrations. Each time they tried to do something, there were more and more delays. Finally one day they decided to ring me, desperate for help.

When I tuned in to the property, I sensed there was a male spirit causing all the havoc. I wasn't wrong because on my way there my GPS kept taking me in circles, as if the old ghost knew that I was on my way to get rid of him. I assume he must have heard the owners talking about me. As soon as I walked into the uncompleted home, I saw an old man spirit standing in front of me, as if trying to stop me in my path. When I asked him what he was doing there he told me he owned the home, that I wasn't welcome, and to get lost. Looking at him, I slowly explained it wasn't his home, that he was dead, and it was time for him to go, as there were loved ones on the other side waiting for him. This took a couple of attempts until finally he must have understood and suddenly disappeared into thin air. According to the woman, the house belonged to an old sea captain who had lived there for years.

Another case was a man wandering around a creek where his car had crashed. He had no idea he was dead. When I spoke to him, he said he could not find his keys and his car was stuck in the river. When I told him that he had died from a head injury, he quickly disappeared as well.

Strong Connection to a Particular Place, Person, or Item

One day a terrified woman rang me and said since she and her husband had moved into a property, everything was going wrong. Her pets had died, there were constant arguments, ill health, and nothing but problems. As she cried hysterically on the phone, she complained of bad smells coming from nowhere, as well as loud, unexplained banging on the wall that constantly kept them awake at night. There were also other unexplainable things going on. Her husband had fallen over and hurt his knee and the whole family kept having bad luck. She was convinced the place was haunted and after hearing how the last owner had died on the property from her neighbor, she was told to call me immediately.

When I arrived and walked into the home, I could smell a horrible rotten energy, like feces in the air. All my hairs stood up on my arms. There was a cold, oppressive feeling that seemed to creep all over my body. No matter how hard I tried, I could not stop burping loudly and repeatedly, despite feeling embarrassed.

The crucifix on my necklace that I had wrapped around my hand proved to be useless: it was ripped out by an invisible force and the beads flew everywhere.

Screaming in fear, the woman and a visiting friend ran hysterically out the front door, leaving me alone in the kitchen. Angry that my beautiful necklace my husband had bought me was now scattered all over the floor in tiny pieces, I called out to the spirit to show himself and told him that I meant no harm and was there to help him. After a few minutes, I saw the outline of a poor male wretched spirit with a noose tied tightly around his neck appear in front of me. When I asked him what he was doing there, he said he did not want to go. He claimed he was not feeling well and wanted to stay in his home where he felt safe. This, of course, was impossible, I told him. He was dead and did not belong there. It was time to go. I also told him nothing bad was going to happen to him and he would get plenty of healing from loved ones in the spirit world that were waiting for him. After repeating myself several times, I finally said a simple Prayer; this seemed to reassure him. As soon as his spirit went, energetically everything seemed to balance itself. Once I had finished, I gave the house a good sage out.

After talking to the women and explaining nothing bad was going to happen now the spirit had gone, the woman's father, who had died a few years before, came through and gave a lasting message, saying her husband would get a new job that would be better.

Ensure the Safety of Particular Loved Ones

When it comes to spirits sticking around to make sure loved ones are safe, the one case that comes to mind was that of an elderly woman I helped, whose sister rang me, convinced her sister's late son was still hanging around. Since his death, the widow had isolated herself and never went anywhere. Her relatives were very worried about what was going on with her and her home. Her son, who had mental health struggles starting in his teenage years, had been living in the house his whole life and spent most of the time locked up in his room. When his late father died from cancer, he spent even more time alone and refused to come out of his room most days. Nobody was surprised when he died from an illness, as he had always been a sickly child and never seemed to get over his father's death.

When I arrived at the house with one of the elderly woman's relatives, I was shocked at the amount of clutter, with every room filled to the rafters with boxes and unnecessary large pieces of wooden furniture. The poor woman, suffering from grief, was a terrible hoarder. Once I sat down and told her I was there to help her, she told me she was very happy as she was convinced her late son's ghost was still living in the house. Every night, without fail, she heard footsteps. Also, the doorbell would ring repeatedly and when she went to open the door, no one was there. She said she heard heavy furniture being dragged around and when she got up in the morning the lounge room would be rearranged. At first, she thought it was an intruder, but when her television kept turning itself on in the middle of the night, she was convinced it was the spirit of her son who always used to watch late-night television.

At the time I was working with an assistant, so it felt very reassuring to have extra help, especially on that occasion, as the whole place was creepy and very dark. When I opened up psychically, we managed to clear a few wandering spirits who were walking around, clueless to what was going on. Everything was going well until I entered the son's room. I sensed a very strong, menacing presence of a spirit person in the corner of the room. The entire room was freezing and dark, and it didn't help that the light switch didn't work.

The window was also shut tight, and the blind pulled down as if it hadn't been opened in years, making it almost impossible to breathe, let alone see anything. The horrible smell in the room made me feel sick to the core and I gasped, nearly choking to get my breath.

My assistant yelled out that he would quickly open the window to get rid of the stale and rank air. Overwhelmed by the ice-cold energy and negativity, I jumped back when I saw what I can only describe as the outline of a young male spirit watching me from the bed. When I told my assistant, he said it was probably the son. I understood then that the spirit was probably worried about his mother being all alone, but it was his time to leave and join his father and loved ones in the spirit world. After repeating myself several times, we both ended up telling the spirit to go. Suddenly, his spirit moved and vanished. No sooner had the spirit left, the darkness dissipated, the smell disappeared, and the room was no longer freezing cold. It just made me sad to think how long he had been trapped and how his mother was powerless to do anything.

Signs You May Have an Earthbound Spirit in Your Place

If you have a lost soul, or earthbound spirit, in your home, it will not go unnoticed, as you will have quite a few issues going on. Ignoring the signs will not help, as these troublesome entities just do not simply go away and it is not your imagination that you may feel drained, scared, or not able to sleep.

All my clients know when something isn't right in their space, as they can feel that something is not right, or feel like they are being attacked and are generally terrified. Once I make contact, I reassure them everything is going to be okay, not to worry, and I will be able to help them straight away. It's amazing the number of people who think the whole concept is rubbish and often they will find out the hard way. I've even heard other mediums say it is rubbish, and this makes me think they can't do the work and don't have the right spirit team. Unless you experience this for yourself, it can come across as far-fetched by many skeptics.

Some of the issues or problems you may encounter are as follows:

Your home will feel ice cold and unpleasant in certain areas, and no matter what you do, the energy will be heavy and unbearable to live in. You will have temperature changes and no explanation why. It may also feel as if you have a black cloud of despair in certain parts of the home and you fill feel miserable and not in control of your life.

You may also have bad smells that are unexplainable, ranging from sickly sweet to the smell of dirty underpants or cigarette smoke and strange perfumes. There may even be a sulfur-like smell. If the entity is a lowly type, it may smell like human excretion or like someone emptied their trash in your house.

You will have constant trouble with electricity and plumbing and things like doorbells, televisions, radios, computers, or other electronic equipment going off by themselves. You may even hear loud pinging sounds in your ear.

Most of the family living in the house will feel drained or unwell, tired, have colds, flus, or other unexplained illnesses. They will also suffer from a lack of sleep. This is the same for pets and children as they are generally more open to energies, very sensitive, and can often feel the negative energy. I don't know how many times I have heard, "My cat keeps staring at the corner of the room for no reason and often yowls," or "My child never sleeps and will never go into a certain room."

In some cases, people will often complain of headaches, feel ungrounded, nauseated, find it hard to make decisions, and may feel anxious for no reason. They may also feel stuck in their lives, confused, have no energy and have problems in almost every aspect of their lives including work, health, and love.

There may be ridiculous continual fights, arguments, or disagreements because of the imbalance of the energy in the house. Being around earthbound spirits can also cause breakups with couples and money problems.

You may feel as if somebody or something invisible is watching you all the time, especially when you are in the shower or having a bath. It may feel as though you are being touched in areas of your body, and, in worse cases, as if someone is trying to smother you, choke you, or strangle you while you sleep. Some people have also complained of being touched in sexual areas, sat on, felt someone lying with them in the bed, or felt pushed.

You may have constant problems doing repairs, renovating a home or making any type of changes, without things going wrong all the time. You will also have problems with councils, neighbors, and it will be almost impossible to sell or make changes to the house because of ridiculous or unexplainable constant delays.

There may be unusual sounds, knocks, rapping on the wall and ceilings and things disappearing for no reason. You may also hear things being dragged in the middle of the night, loud footsteps, or the phone ringing and nobody on the other end when you answer. You may also think you can hear muffled voices in the background of a phone call.

You will feel drained all the time, as earthbound spirits need energy to stay in our world. They will suck your energy to stay here, like parasites, so they need to be passed on. So many times I have heard, "I know I have a spirit woman living with me, so I stay home all the time." For lost souls to be here is karmically not okay, as they do not belong here and need to go back into the spirit world.

Nightmares are very common and often indicate there is a negative spirit in the home that needs to be crossed. These nightmares may vary in degree and duration and over time can get worse, as it is the lost soul begging for your attention. You may dream you are being chased, murdered, attacked, kicked, suffocated, and be left with a terrible feeling of dread when you wake up.

You may have a few ghost orbs floating around your place, which are different from other lighter orbs. Ghost orbs are bigger, thicker, and denser in appearance than spirit orbs or nature orbs. I have seen a few as large as the size of a tennis ball. These ghost orbs appear to have a thicker texture but are harder to see and are not as common as the spirit or nature orbs that just seem to appear naturally. Some are also black in appearance and look ominous. Although harmless, ghost orbs can be disruptive, considering that you are dealing with a lost soul.

Some of the symptoms of ghost orbs include items disappearing, pictures or heavy furniture moved, or objects flying through the air for no reason. You may find objects that are not yours appear in your house, such as medicine or coins for example. It is very common to see elevators running and operating themselves, with doors closing and opening but no one is there. You may see dark shadows out of the corner of your eye, or something flash past suddenly in the distance.

Physical reactions are common, such as feeling nauseous, hair standing on edge, or continuously burping without any control. There may also be a terrible feeling of something invisible pushing down on you, trying to suffocate you, lying next to you, or touching you

It may also feel as if negative energy is unrelenting. Things may often go wrong, problems will come up at work, and it may seem like you are having constant, terrible bad luck, as if you are cursed.

Do Spirits Follow You?

Spirits can follow people and they do, especially the wandering spirits. Over the years, I have experienced years of weird and strange paranormal things going on, with a supernatural theme continuing in my life today. The one thing I have learned is to use protection every day, use boundaries, and make sure I am grounded and focused and paying full attention when I go to busy places, like hospitals, haunted venues, and clients' homes. It is important to make sure I don't bring home unwanted guests into my own home. I don't know how many times I found unwanted spirits sitting in the back of my car, like the time I worked at a very haunted venue for the weekend only to come home and have my glass shower screen shatter the next morning by an unwanted dark shadow. Horrified, I never told the husband and was so lucky we had the home fully insured. He would be totally petrified if he knew what I saw and truly angry if he knew the truth about what had really happened. The sound of the loud explosion still rings in my ears and is a constant reminder to do all the normal checks when going to these places.

I also remember helping a dear friend, a medium who used to drive all around the countryside and interstate, doing spirit shows and readings in homes for large groups of people. He was always complaining how his car was constantly breaking down and how he was always spending all his money on the continuous problems. One day he got the shock of his life when I cleared his car after lunch and told him he had three spirits sitting in the back seat of his car. He laughed and agreed it was probably true, as he was always freezing cold even on the hottest of days and never had to use the car's air conditioner. These days he is always paying attention with his protection and making sure he doesn't pick up any free rides for lost souls.

CHAPTER 3

TYPES OF SPIRITS
AND WHERE TO FIND THEM

I have encountered many types of spirits or lost souls in my work of spirit rescue and hauntings. They are all very different and handled in different ways. The one thing I have discovered with my work is that spirits love busy places. The busier the location, the more spirits you will discover.

Connected to the Location

Earthbound spirits are spirits that have died on a property or lived there once while alive. For unknown reasons they are confused and have an attachment or believe they are still alive, as they do not understand or comprehend that they are actually dead. These lost souls have not moved on, so to speak, so they come back again to stay and haunt the property. Earthbound spirits are the most difficult to remove as they have no intention to leave. This causes many problems over time, making it almost impossible for new inhabitants to live peacefully, especially if the new occupants want to make changes. Earthbound spirits don't like strangers in their space and will make life a misery for the living.

Renovations in any shape or form can be a nightmare with constant and frustrating delays. After all, earthbound spirits believe it's their home and are probably angry or confused as to who these other people in *their* home are and why are they living in *their* home.

To clear these spirits takes a lot of time and persuasion. Even after telling the spirits they are dead, to open their eyes, and cross over into the light, these spirits can be very stubborn and often will not want to go. In some cases when you smoke out the property, even several times, the stubborn spirit or spirits will simply go outside, walk around the property, and then come back again once the air is clear.

Ross and Amy

One case study that comes to mind is when I was called out to a brand-new home where the inhabitants could not find peace and were constantly at each other's throats arguing. After a while, they were convinced there must have been some type of malevolent energy present, as the new home, which had once been a warehouse, had been recently redeveloped. The space felt sad the moment you stepped in the door.

Thinking at first it was just their imagination, once they moved in the house, there was turmoil and constant problems. After a few months the unhappy couple even spoke of divorce, their children moved out, and they fought with their families because of their heated arguments. They were also frustrated and sad when their dog disappeared; he was an important part of the once happy family. If it wasn't for a kind neighbor who understood the struggles with earthbound spirits, they would have probably ended the marriage. The couple tried smoking out the house with sage, per a suggestion by the neighbor, but to no avail, because after about a week the bad luck returned. When I got called to the property, the place seemed clear until I went in the basement where I discovered five earthbound spirits hiding in a cupboard. It took a while to release them. They appeared frightened and I could see the outlines of the spirits, all huddling together in a bunch, feeling very confused and scared. I told them out loud that they were dead, it was time to go. Instantly they disappeared, leaving a very light energy behind as they crossed into the light that I had called down. After I had finished, I asked the new owners if there had been a fire in the history of the property because I had a sense of smoke and kept seeing red flames in my mind, which must have been some kind of psychic imprint or knowing. Looking confused at first, they said yes, but it had taken place many years before and the property had been vacant for years. The whole thing was very sad. As for the new owners, they never had any problems after the confused spirits were crossed and they were very grateful for the intervention. Everybody, spirits and those alive, deserves a happy and peaceful life.

Wandering Spirits

Wandering spirits are earthbound spirits that are lost, but they move around, away from their home. These spirits may end up following you, jumping in your car, riding with you in the train, collecting en masse where there are crowds, and coming home if you have been to a haunted venue or traveled past where they died.

I don't know how many times I've had spirits jump in the back of my car and hitch a ride. Because these spirits love to be a nuisance, you may begin to have car problems if they are not cleared. They never tend to stay in one place and generally like to congregate where there are lots of people. You often find them in groups or in bunches together. It's not common to find them alone, as all these lost souls live off our energy.

In some cases, I have cleared the earthbound spirit from people's homes or properties and found wandering spirits as well. I have also cleared houses where someone has been in a road accident and decided to occupy a nearby home. Wandering spirits may also hang out around a busy highway or where there has been an accident, murder, or hanging. A lot of these types of lost spirits have died suddenly. They can be a real nuisance, just like all earthbound spirits, as they do not understand they are dead. They are lost and confused in an astral world, looking for some type of comfort. Wandering spirits don't need to be pitied but rather need to be sent off for their own healing.

I have experienced these types of spirits many times in my work, from ordinary people that have had problems, to mediums, healers, or psychics that seem to attract these lost souls if they don't close down or cloak their energies. A few of my sitters have experienced this type of phenomenon and I have taught them how to protect themselves, cloak and bring down the white light, and command the often-confused spirit to leave and to cross into the spirit world.

Bill

One of my worst cases involving wandering spirits was that of a prison officer who had worked in a jail for many years. Bill was a good person and helped and encouraged many of the inmates with rehabilitation to improve their lives on the outside when they left jail. While working in the jail, he would complain he often brought home spirits of the deceased that had been sick and died in jail. He said he felt weird, negative energies from some of the hardened criminals that had died. He also told me he was convinced some of the inmates had come back to the jail as spirits when they had died on the outside, as things would go on all the time that were inexplainable. As one could imagine, there would be a lot of dark energies around some of these hardened criminals who were all confined to small, compact places. When Bill, through the help of a friend, contacted me, I helped him a couple of times in his house when things were bad and there were lost souls and negative energy to clear. He was always grateful. His family was fed up, sick of putting up with dad's ghosts, and nagged him to get help. One day he told me he was convinced "the bastards" were jumping in his car and following him. So, laughing to myself and understanding his frustration, I showed him how to stop it and how to protect and cloak himself when he was at work. Everything changed for him when I explained how to stop this and clear his space.

Poltergeist

The word *poltergeist* comes from the German words *poltern*—meaning to rumble, bluster, or jangle—and *geist*—meaning spirit. *Poltern* can also be used in describing an act of speech: speaking loudly and abrasively. In some cases, clients will complain about whistling or screeching noises keeping them awake all night. Although *poltergeist* literally means "noisy spirit," a poltergeist is neither a spirit nor a ghost, according to paranormal and parapsychology experts. Usually described as an invisible force and entity, the nature of poltergeists has long been a subject of debate within paranormal circles. This can apply to all types of lost spirits, due to an attachment, and is very easy to recognize when objects move around by themselves. When I see this type of spirit activity, the lost spirit is generally strong enough to be able to move objects or scratch people's bodies. In my early years with his work, I have been pushed and thrown into the air by angry spirits. Now I often take a team of other rescuers for protection and assistance. If I do a remote scan of the property before physically visiting, I generally have a good feeling of what I am to expect. These days, I like to use remote viewing and rescue with this type of spirit, as it is less confronting and much easier on my energy. Once I have finished with a remote viewing, I instruct the client on how to smoke out the place a couple of times, with good results.

Some of the Problems Involved

Objects such as keys, clothes, food, or other belongings, may just disappear into thin air or move around for no apparent reason, sometimes right in front of you. Also, in many cases, you will have an uncanny feeling that something with a ghost-like nature is definitely living in your home. These beings will always make themselves known, whether you believe in such things or not. Experiencing poltergeists is something you will never forget as it is so confrontational and proof to all non-believers that lost souls do indeed exist.

Larger objects, such as furniture, which are often difficult for beings that are alive to move, may be moved or dragged around. Objects may also fly through the air, right in front of your eyes.

You may experience strange pungent smells, such as cigarettes, perfumes, or other strange odors that don't seem to have a source. Some clients have even found the smell to follow them to work or other places outside the home.

Electrical items, such as a radio or television, may be turned off and on for no apparent reason at any time day. All types of spirits love electricity. You may experience a shaking bed, objects lifted up in the air, or strange unexplained phenomena.

You may hear unexplained noises such as knocks, rapping on walls, constant footsteps, dragging sounds, or walking and running up and down the corridors. A very common problem is the telephone ringing all the time but finding no one there when answering., The doorbell may ring all hours of the day and night, but when you get up to investigate, nothing is there.

You may wake up with scratches or strange marks on your body for no apparent reason, or, in some cases, feel someone watching you all the time or sitting or sleeping next to you.

You may feel something touching your private parts or wanting to have sex with you, which may be a sign of an incubus. An incubus is a demon in a male form that likes to sleep with women or men and engage in sexual activity. A female counter part is a succubus. If left to stay, this being can cause deterioration of physical and mental health. Once these unwanted spirits are recognized, they are removed, do not come back, and the energy is restored to harmony and balance.

In some of the cases I have worked on, the poltergeists can be spirit children that are attracted to a family or children in a home and like to cause havoc. I once also worked on a case where a lost spirit, right before our eyes, lifted a small table laden with tea and delicate small cakes. The couple I was working with screamed as things flew everywhere and crashed on the floor. It was a spirit boy who had killed himself and was fighting with his father at the time of his death. Once I spoke to him and told him all was forgiven, he disappeared and never came back again. The clients thanked me and said they were no longer fearful and were very grateful. They looked forward to a good night's sleep without any interference, no loud noises to wake them up in the middle of the night. They were exhausted and had had enough drama for a whole lifetime.

Mandy

Another case was of a woman thinking the unfriendly spirit that she must have picked up along the way was her late father. Feeling sorry for her late father and thinking his spirit was around, she invited it in and was soon attacked. There were scratches on her back and she often felt as if she was being strangled in her sleep. Her house began to feel ice cold. The client also felt sad and tired all the time. She was attacked on a nightly basis in her bedroom unless she left the light on to deter it. In the end, she was too scared to go to sleep and felt as if she was dying. Even after I cleared the unsavory spirit, I heard from some friends she still found it hard to go to sleep without a light on, even though nothing has happened since the clearing.

Shadow Spirits

Shadow spirits are a collective of dark, menacing souls, and sometimes described as a type of phenomenon. They are described as having humanoid features with red eyes, and appearing long, black, and thin, sometimes looking cartoonish One weird thing about shadow spirits is they often wear some type of top hat. They seem to operate alone, slide on walls when you are trying to get rid of them, and will refuse to go into the light. I remove these awful dark souls by either sending them to where they came from or sending them into the earth. Shadow spirits are horrible entities that do not belong in our realm and can cause a lot of harm to a young child. They mostly hide under beds of children who have suffered nightmares for as long as they can remember and are too scared to even sleep in a room on their own. Even when the family have moved to another home, the dark spirit will follow and continue to taunt the child like prey. Some people call thses spirits "boogey men."

I first came across this type of phenomenon when I attended a trance group with other mediums and sitters many years ago, in my early development days. While taking a break from the class and talking to a friend while she smoked a cigarette, I unexpectedly saw a strange group of weird, tallish, dark beings standing together in a row against a wall in the next-door building. Not believing my eyes and thinking I was imagining things, I whispered to the others to quickly have a look to see what they thought. No sooner had I done this than the other mediums confirmed my thoughts and said what I was thinking: those dark beings I was seeing were very dark souls that appeared to have menacing, cold, creepy energies. Scanning the area, we had a closer look and saw these dark beings all appeared tall, humanoid in shape, and they seemed to constantly distort into different sizes. A few also had red eyes. We all agreed they had some type of intelligence, given that they saw us watching them. Once the beings discovered they were being watched, they immediately stopped bobbing around and seemed to look back at us in a menacing way. If they hadn't appeared like silly cartoon characters in what looked like top hats and dark onesies suits, we would have run for the hills. Feeling very brave, I told the group I would move them on with my spirit team. As I approached these beings, I felt a coldness run all down my body. As I commanded them to leave and go into the light, nothing happened. It felt like we were in a standoff, as the shadow spirits stood their ground. Frustrated and not knowing what to do, I was about to turn around and leave when I heard my guide say, "Tell them to leave, never return and to go back to where they came from."

No sooner had I yelled this out very loudly, they all disappeared into the cold night and the place emptied and felt peaceful again. This was a valuable lesson that dark spirits will never go into the light. The whole experience, like anything you do to a spirit, was a learning curve. It was my first introduction of working with this type of phenomenon, so I was grateful for the experience. I recall not being able to sleep that night and kept checking under my bed to see if anything had followed me home.

When I and the other mediums informed the teacher teaching the trance class, he said he was not surprised. He was convinced there was some type of criminal activity going on in the property as the energy always felt dark and the people there he believed were hardened criminals. He went on to tell us he even believed they may have had a meth lab and dealt with drugs because there was constantly traffic going on, with endless people dropping in at all hours. He said he just kept to himself but always put a protection on his boundary. I still to this day do not understand why he even lived there.

After this incident, I did not feel comfortable attending the trance course because I was opening up my energies in such a toxic place. That night I made a mental note that I would not be going back. In hindsight, it all made sense, as I never felt comfortable at the class but the experience also showed me a new type of dark energy I would experience in my work.

Several years later, I attended a conference and listened to a presenter who spoke of shadow spirits being an alien race. I have no idea if this is true but can only describe my own experience and what I saw. Once the entity was told to go back to where it belonged, it seemed to work for me, as none of my clients have ever complained or called me back again with the same problem.

Orbs

Have you ever noticed tiny orbs of light darting around certain places, such as natural spaces, workspaces, or at home? When you are aware of this type of phenomenon, it is easy for most people to see these beautiful tiny little lights, found in many shapes and sizes, moving before your eyes.

You don't have to be a psychic to see them. You just need to be aware they exist, as they are spirit energy and are all around us at certain times. Once you are aware of orbs, it is easy to catch their image with a camera. People may joke and think you are pulling their leg and say it is just a piece of dust on your camera lens. Once they see orbs for themselves, they are likely to be as delighted as you are, as they can look quite extraordinary.

Orbs are spirit life forms that travel around and are believed to be the human soul or life force of those that once inhabited a physical body here on earth. Sometimes, depending on the size of the orb, you may also be able to see a tiny face inside.

Ghost Orbs

Ghost orbs are bigger, thicker, and denser in appearance than spirit orbs or nature orbs, which we'll talk about next. In my work of spirit rescue, I have seen a few the size of tennis balls. On closer inspection, ghost orbs appear to have a thicker texture and can appear in a range of different colors, but are mainly dark in color. These orbs are lost souls that have not crossed over to the other side. Unfortunately, in most cases, these lost souls or ghosts have no idea they are dead when you talk to them. Their confusion means you will not get an explanation as to why they did not cross over or refused to go when it was their time. Although harmless, ghost orbs can be disruptive and make life difficult as they not only draw on our energy but also can play havoc by disrupting events at your home or business. If they are living in your home, they will make themselves known because they want your attention. These orbs need to be smoked out or crossed over.

Spirit Orbs

Spirit orbs are usually lighter in color when compared to ghost orbs and can vary in shape and size. Some appear as tiny pin pricks or can be as large as an apple or an orange. I see these as tiny shining lights that glisten like stars. They are beautiful to look at and some people may call them angels. Spirit orbs are our loved ones or friends from the other side. They may also be healing guides, angels, or spirit doctors. The spirit doctors or healing orbs mainly frequent places where people do spiritual healing. These orbs are totally harmless and capable of continuing a full spiritual existence on the other side with full mental and emotional faculties intact, unlike ghost orbs. They are also able to communicate to loved ones or get a message across via a medium. They may do this through dreams or via what I call "signposts," such as music, animals, birds, smells or simply feelings. Their message is always the same—to let their loved ones know that they are safe and have made it to the other side. By communicating in this way, our loved ones are letting us know that love and life are eternal and that they still care for us. They may also have a message for us about what is going on in our own lives. Our loved ones who have crossed over are living in a vast, more expansive space that can be similar to Earth, but without the need for the comforts we have here, such as food or sex. These types of orbs have a vibration that is on a higher level compared to those living on this plane. Once they have done their healing on the other side, they are bathed in pure unconditional love from, what is called, the "source of all things."

Nature Orbs

How many of you have seen beautiful lights outside in your garden or in nature? These are usually nature orbs and can vary in shape and size like the spirit orbs. They seem to accumulate in large groups, and you usually see a whole lot of these transparent, shining orbs bobbing up and down all over the place out in nature or above water. These nature orbs are elemental spirits and are incredibly healing. There are four types of these elementals: salamanders, sylphs, earth spirits, and undines. Each is different but they all coexist in harmony. Nature orbs are active in our great forests or anywhere on the planet where there is an abundance of grass, flowers, trees, water, or wildlife. I have seen many undines, or water fairies, around rivers, lakes, waterfalls, or rocky ponds in the form of little lights or opaque orbs. They dislike human interference, such as the dumping of garbage, and can become disruptive if too many changes are made to a yard space or a natural environment. I always seek permission from nature orbs if I want to make changes to my landscape in my garden. It is also a good idea to make a tiny fairy garden in your yard as the nature spirits will always heal sick plants if you place them there. Place a birdbath with water in your garden to increase harmony and bring in good fortune.

Common Places to Find Lost Souls

Earthbound spirits and lost souls, which have not yet found closure with leaving the earth plane, will generally congregate or linger around where there are large groups of people. This could include places such as hotels, hospitals, railway stations, brothels, old schools, clubs, battlefields, shopping centers, airports, sports centers, graveyards, casinos, jails, refugee camps, bridges, some murder scenes, occasionally busy highways, or places where there have been terrible accidents or disasters. I have seen large numbers of lost souls in these places, so be aware and always remember to protect yourself, especially if you are sensitive to energies. Lost souls need our energy or body heat to draw from to be here on Earth. It's very seldom that you will find a lost soul or wandering spirit at a lonely graveyard unless there are large groups of people at a funeral or on a paranormal tour.

Generally, when we die, our spirit transitions directly into the spirit realm. Mediums are able to make contact with the deceased as soon as the person dies and leaves their earthly body. As experienced and trained mediums, such as myself, we are able to give evidence of their passing, how they died, and help deliver messages in great detail. Some loved ones will also talk about their family, partners, children, food, or even their gardens. Others may give information of what is going on in the lives of the living: the living's past, present, and future, right down to problems, worries, and outcomes. The best thing of all is that these souls can give the message they have survived their transition and are safe and well in spirit, which is in another dimension just a hands-length away. When we receive messages from our loved ones in spirit, we receive love, comfort, healing, and, more importantly, closure. Love is eternal and goes way beyond the bounds of human experience.

Unfortunately, a small minority of spirits stay behind and wander aimlessly around until there is help by spirit intervention via their guide, guardian angel, or spirit rescuer, which will assist with the crossing over process. This is because, as I have said, they are unable to comprehend that they are dead.

As far back as I can remember, I have had so many of these scary, paranormal, ghostly occurrences, which I thought and, naively, believed were normal. My family never witnessed or experienced anything I saw and had no idea what I was talking about when I tried to tell them about my experiences. The local church I attended as a small child didn't help or want to know either. After my confirmation, I told a visiting evangelist from church I could see dead people, or ghosts, and knew certain things that would happen in the future. I was told I had the devil in me and was made an outcast, never to return. At the time, I was too scared to tell my mother what the woman said and refused to ever go back again. It was a terrible feeling to lose my spiritual family and made me more paranoid that perhaps I was evil. Those feelings changed when I threw myself into the local beach culture, which was a very liberating place to be as a young teenager. The lesson taught me to be strong, move on, and not to tell people too much about myself and my secrets.

We all have our lessons and learning in life for our spiritual time on earth, and, as it turned out spirit had other plans for me. Once I turned seventeen and had my driving license, I was taken under the care of a very kindly woman, an English medium, who trained me in her spiritual church. For that duration of time in my life, she taught myself and others, how to use our special gifts. She told us our training would be ongoing for the rest of our lives until our guides took over and became the teachers. That wonderful woman offered, selflessly, so much love and guidance at a very hard and difficult time in my life. For that I am forever grateful and humbled.

From that point on I have moved onwards and understand that the spirit world is a mass consciousness of love and light and healing. I am forever grateful for everything I get to experience as it is never boring. When you work for spirit, spirit puts food on your table, a roof over your head and love in your heart. The journey is ever constant and constantly changing.

Here are a few stories I have collected over the years from hundreds of case studies of where souls may congregate. Anyone can experience a ghost or lost soul because it affects people from all walks of life.

Houses

Most people I know have experienced a ghost or two in a home, business, or similar space sometime in their life. They can be anywhere—the city, the country—any areas where there are people. Haunted houses will always have a menagerie of spirits and often an array of ghost orbs. They can vary in color and may appear, depending on whether the spirit is malevolent, black or white. These types of energies need to go and don't belong in our realm of the living. Lost souls, wandering spirits, and earthbound spirits can be heard by the client I may be working with. Clients may also hear sounds such as pounding, footsteps in corridors, banging on walls, zaps of electricity, or any other disembodied sounds. These sounds wil often scare the daylights out of the people. The sounds will often be reported by the client as a problem, keeping them up at night. As one can imagine, this causes disharmony and disruption to the natural balance of the home. Most of the haunted houses I have been to have a history of problems. This can go on for years unless the energy is cleared. The disruptions caused by lost souls will not stop or change if the old house is tore down and a new home built. If the lost souls are not removed from the property, the same problems will continue and, in some cases, even intensify.

The Troublesome Flower Shop

Tom and Jeff were a lovely couple that owned an older building in an urban area that was used for their garden business. From the moment they moved in, they had ongoing problems and were convinced their building was unlucky and full of some type of negative energy. No matter how hard they tried to get their business going, nothing worked. This was unusual as all the other business around them were highly profitable, always busy, and people seemed to always flock around. However, for some strange reason, customers never stepped foot inside their floral shop.

After great expectations of a wonderful business and spending a bit of money on hiring a feng shui specialist, everything seemed to go well for a while. However, within months, the business crumbled again and nothing they did or tried seemed to help to improve the energy. In the end, they gave up their dream and put the business on the market. They had enough of trying to make ends meet and were tired of nothing working. However, at the last minute, the couple contacted me as a last resort through a mutual friend. They were hoping that I would be able to try and sort things out so they could at least get a good price for their shop when they placed it on the market.

Stepping through the door of the old building, I smiled knowingly, as even though the Master had placed cures in all the right places, it was obvious to me the bad energy was still there. The energy kept hitting me in the stomach like a baseball bat. The more I walked around the space, the sicker I felt. It felt like a darkness and a negative energy were hitting me, relentlessly, right in pit my stomach. The whole space felt horrendous, and it was obvious there was a lot of spirit activity present, which was causing the problems and the troubles in the floral shop. The Master's cures, though very insightful and very good, were unfortunately blocked because of the stagnant paranormal energy. After walking around and clearing the heavy energy, sending it off into portholes of light, I finally made my way down to the basement of the building and found the real reason for the disruptive energy. Huddled together in a tiny cupboard behind a trap door within a wall were two wretched lost spirits, which had been murdered many years ago. The shop was in a trendy old area of the city where crime gangs once reigned, and it appeared these lost souls were victims of those crime gangs. The bodies were most likely moved at some point as there were no bones or evidence of bodies, but the spirits were still there, trapped in some type of time warp.

When I told Tom and Jeff what I had found, they just stared at me in disbelief. They said they remembered that the older building did have a bit of a reputation and was even rented by a bikie gang for many years where they sold drugs, made deals, and held meetings. It was very sad to experience this, as I could feel so many emotions of pain, agony, and terror, making me believe these souls had truly suffered.

Opening up, we all joined hands and stood in a circle while I said a prayer under my breath. I asked for protection for everyone and gave a tribute to the lost spirits and any other spirits that had suffered in this horrible energy. Within seconds, the whole room suddenly lit up like a Christmas tree and began to fill with an amazing, bright light, full of what seemed like a thousand or so healing angels, all singing and reaching out to the spirits to take them home. After a few minutes, we all stood back after closing down, stunned, watching in disbelief as the heavy, depressing energy that had been lingering for so long disappeared without a trace.

Time heals all and within two months of the spirit rescue, Tom rang me up, thanked me a thousand times for the experience, and happily informed me that the building had sold for the exact money he and Jeff hoped for, and that they had bought a property in the country.

The Gilded Cage

My friends Lisa and Stephen had just sold their home and decided to rent a beautiful mansion, with all the trappings, that was over a hundred years old and near the sea. At first, the family settled in well, but before too long, things started to go wrong. I received a phone call from my friend, who was in tears. She was convinced the house was haunted. It had funny smells, the rooms were always freezing, everyone seemed to have the flu constantly, and she felt as though there was an invisible, dark force watching her all the time, making her feel scared and anxious. It seemed as though this dark force was acting beyond the mansion because every time the family attempted to buy a different property, something would go wrong and it seemed as though they were on hold all the time. After a period of time, Lisa also said she became depressed, never had energy to do much of the work she loved, and the kids were arguing and fighting all the time.

One afternoon, all her fears came to a head when her eldest son said he saw two ghostly figures walking down the upstairs corridor and into his bedroom. Too scared to go back into his room—he swore he saw them sitting on the bed—he camped every night on his parents' bedroom floor with his doona and refused to go back into his room unless accompanied by someone.

After Lisa called me, I went to the house. It was a massive, old, four-story building that faced the sea and was exposed to the elements. It looked eerie and reminded me of an old fortress, very majestic in its day but felt as though it had a lot of history. From the moment I walked in, I could sense there were many lost spirits there. I could feel invisible, silent eyes staring down at me from the stairs above. Wrapping myself with white light and a blue cloak for extra protection, I walked around the home while my friends sat downstairs in the kitchen, too scared to accompany me. Before too long, many more spirits gathered around me and some of them seemed confused and angry. As I smoked the home with sage, I called on them to go as they did not belong there. When I went to the boy's bedroom, I found the two spirits he was talking about, hiding in a cupboard. Everything was going well until I reached the basement. It felt negative and extremely sad. It was then that I understood the problem. My spirit guide told me that there had been a fire when the home was first built. An entire family and their servants had been killed when they became trapped and the building collapsed. When I asked Lisa if she knew this, she confirmed and said she had heard of the tragedy but that it had happened long ago.

Calling on all the lost spirits to leave, I imagined a porthole of great light coming down from the heavens. I also told the lost spirits, ever so gently, not to be afraid; it was time for them to be free and to go home where all their loved ones would be waiting. Within a matter of seconds, the energy shifted. It felt incredibly lighter, brighter and all the negativity that was present disappeared. In its place was a loud silence with tiny shimmering lights, indicating the spirits had left.

Yelling with joy, Lisa, who was at my side as the spirits left, appeared stunned. She kept repeating she had never experienced anything like this in her life. Laughing with relief, she told me she was overjoyed to know the spirits that were trapped were finally free and everything in her life would now go back to normal.

Three weeks later, she rang me up and said, very happily, that she and her family had finally found their forever home and could not wait to renovate and get back to family life.

My First Home

After setting up home with my second husband, our life was very harmonious as we worked very well together, and it was easy saving money. Eventually, we bought a small home in a very trendy inner suburb of the city. It was formally owned by an elderly couple who had lived in the house for many years. Because they had no children, we inherited what was left of their estate—a collection of bits and bobs that included everything from an old commode to pictures of kittens on a wall, painted a shiny yellow with bright red trimmings. We also inherited a very old walking frame that must have belonged to the widow. I did not think for a minute it could be haunted, but there were a few red flags in the beginning that I ignored. After a while, strange and unexplainable things were going on inside our home. Every day, just when I was about to cook dinner for the family, something very strange would happen. As soon as the clock hit five in the afternoon, a stinking, sickly smell of urine would manifest from nowhere and appear for a few minutes as a wet puddle on the lounge room floor, then disappear. The smell was so strong and so rancid that it made me feel sick. The awful smell would gradually waft its way from room to room and no matter where you were in the house you could always smell it.

At first, I thought it was the cat. Scolding him, I put him outside dozens of times. I'm not surprised he was furious with me as he was innocent and being blamed for something he didn't do. I'm sure he could sense there was a spirit there, as animals are very psychic. I remember how he would often growl and howl at nothing all the time.

After a while, my eldest daughter, who was only ten years old at the time, would yell and scream with annoyance that the awful smell was back and kept telling me to do something about it. Frustrated, one day I nearly fell over backward when I saw a ghostly woman walk right past me and through a doorway. I had just come home from work, and from that point on the ghostly apparition seemed to make it a habit to visit around that time every day, followed by the smell of urine. When I told our neighbor about what was going on, she confirmed the woman who had previously lived in the house struggled with incontinence before she passed. I also remember hearing a dragging noise occasionally, which might have been the spirit lady using her old walking frame.

It hadn't struck me that she could still be in the house, as the house had a welcoming feel to it. Except for the strong smell of urine on the carpet, she never bothered us, and we all used to just joke about the incident. As far as we knew she was harmless, but probably just a little curious about what was going on in her well-loved home, as we had made so many changes when we moved into the place and there were always renovations going on. However, over time, events of a ghostly nature increased and it was apparent things were not right. It started getting really weird when things began to move around by themselves, such as a cup being moved, doors closing, lights going on and off, and ordinary items disappearing into thin air. When this happened, I decided I had enough, and it was time for her to go and join her husband on the other side.

This was, again, an early lesson in my spirit rescue practice to understand: lost souls and earthbound spirits do not belong here and need to be moved on. They can become pests after a while and often do not like it when you change the style of their previous living space. Feeling sorry for them by keeping them earthbound will do nothing for their spiritual progression as a soul. Once I understood what was going on, I told her it was time to go and sent her over, where I am sure her husband was waiting very patiently for her to join him. Lost souls are not a novelty, joke, or pet to be kept to show off to our friends and family.

Brothels

Over the years, I have also been asked to clear out brothels when the sex workers are experiencing trouble of a supernatural nature. After I have smoked out a brothel property and cleared any unwanted spirit visitors I always show the women or men how to protect themselves, as they are working with all types of energies. One woman, who appeared very unwell, had the spirit of her old boyfriend, who had died of a drug overdose, living in her room she used at the brothel. Once I told her I could sense him and saw a gray shadow of him lying in her bed, she said she knew, felt sorry for him because he had died of a drug overdose and could not stop pining for him every day. This was exhausting for her. Thinking it was her fault, she continued to sleep with him, felt him touching her, and encouraged him in her imagination to stay. This, of course, was wrong, and over time, it made her mentally, emotionally, and psychically sick.

When I confirmed he was there, as the dark energy in the room made me feel sick to the core, I told him, very sternly, he did not belong here any longer and he had to cross. After a few minutes of gentle but firm persuasion, he finally went. All of the dark, pungent, thick negative energy dispersed slowly from the room into two large columns of light I had energetically created in the center of the room. Finally, after smoking out the room, I told her to open the windows and to let the light and the warmth of the sun's rays in. This would help with the healing process and encourage good chi energy to bring more peace and harmony in. Thanking me for helping her, she started crying and said she had been feeling numb for a very long time, did not know what to do, and felt totally out of her depth. Giving her a huge hug, I told her we did the right thing, as he was suffering and did not belong here. I told her that trying to help him had caused her so much grief. I also suggested she catch up with some much needed sleep, as the poor woman looked like she hadn't slept in weeks. It was time for her to start looking after herself in a healthier way.

Not long after this incident, I heard from the woman who owned the brothel. She said the place had improved, business was good, and all the girls were happy. She also said the worker I had helped improved, she no longer looked ghostly pale, and she was happy again.

Boarding Houses

Over the years I have crossed over a lot of lost souls in huge buildings all over the place. I have seen people get sick for no reason and have nothing but bad luck in their lives, mostly due to ghosts drawing on their energy if not crossed. One of my biggest cases was that of an old boarding house that used to be some type of school. I was called in by a developer renovating the property, whose wife was familiar with my work. This developer was having numerous ongoing problems: struggles with the local council, enormous costs, and hopeless trades people that never showed up to do work. The day I visited the property, I had only one assistant with me, a dowser to help me locate and move the spirit's onward. I had an idea of what we would be working with, as I had done a remote viewing before arriving in person. I knew there would be a few more spirits present, as I had seen clusters of them in my morning meditation the day we planned to visit the property. It took ages to clear the house of fifteen earthbound spirits and I was very grateful I had made the decision to take an extra hand, as the work can be exhausting working with that many earthbound spirits. After we cleared the huge building, the developer, a very cynical and judgmental non-believer, learned a new lesson. He could not believe what he witnessed and was speechless. He kept thanking me when we left and apologized for his rudeness. When he got the approval from the council about three weeks later, his wife rang me and said they were both over the moon as the place was rented to full capacity.

Hotels, Clubs, Old Theaters

I have yet to find a hotel in the world that does not have a ghost or two. As far back as I can remember I have always had problems when traveling and staying in hotels, unless I clear the room and protect myself, especially overnight. This is because buildings have and carry a long history of other people's baggage, and when it builds up, it slowly leeches into the walls and carpet, energetically infiltrating the whole space unless it's cleared.

As I've mentioned before, lost souls like to congregate where there are lots of people to whom they can attach themselves. How many times have you walked into a place and felt, right away, that the place and vibes did not feel right? The older the building is, the more likely you are to have a feeling like this. Even if a new building is built, if its constructed on an old site without it being cleared, the same problems will continue to occur in the new building, as the lost spirits have not moved on.

In a hotel, usually the first people to complain of weird things going on will be the staff that work there, regardless of their personal beliefs about supernatural phenomena. Things to expect in a situation like this include weird smells, doors opening and closing, changes in temperature, lifts going up and down all night by themselves, lights flickering, water and sewage problems, electrical problems, clocks not working, a sickly feeling that something does not feel right giving you cold chills or goose bumps, and electrical equipment turning on and off. Most likely there will also be complaints from irritated and scared guests mentioning weird noises or an inability to sleep because they felt something in the room with them—all signs something is wrong of a paranormal nature. The hotel will most likely start to lose business and visitors will not come back. Any spas, wellness centers, or gift shops within a hotel will also struggle with lost business.

I don't know how many hotels I have stayed in where some extremely pesky spirit has been drawn to me because of my psychic light and watched me—a stark-naked, middle-aged woman—trying to have a bath, which tells me the lost soul has not let go of their earthly pleasures. When this has happened, I'm not impressed in the slightest, as I've had to submerge myself in bubbles while desperately searching for a towel before sending the troublesome spirit off. This type of behavior enrages me because the spirit in question has no time for anyone's modesty. I have also been kept up all night by TVs being turned on and off, radios playing songs, and things moving around on their own.

The Hotel Conference

Once working at a conference in a very old, haunted hotel, I could sense and smell—with my nose working overtime—so many lost souls throughout the place while walking around its corridors. Sometimes, in places filled with so many spirits, it's like a memory land, as some of the spirits appear in old fashion clothing. The old building the conference was in must have been grand in its day, and I am sure it held many memories of yesteryear. I did sense a lot of spirit activity of a paranormal nature: the place was buzzing with invisible energy, my nose kept running, I was burping softly to myself, and I saw flashes on the side of my eyes indicating there were many spirits present. Nothing of a sinister nature was evident, so I breathed deeply and looked forward to the weekend, thinking that so long as I was protected, I was safe. I planned to just keep to myself; I had checked and sealed my room with white light to keep visiting spirits out and I had no plans of doing any rescue work, only aiming to concentrate on my busy schedule for the weekend. Hopefully any lost souls would just keep away.

Everything was going really well until the second day when a client, a good psychic I was training for the weekend, had a weird spirit hovering around her energy all the time. The dark shadow seemed to keep popping in and out, moving closer, then disappearing again. While everyone was under doing a deep meditation, which I had instructed, I had the chance to give the woman a good scan of her aura. I was gobsmacked when I could clearly see the outline of a ghostly spirit standing almost on top of her, like a thick, dark shadow. Somehow it did not feel right to me and sensing foul play, I asked the woman discreetly while on our coffee break, "Who is the spirit man hanging around you all the time and what is he doing?"

Embarrassed and looking stunned, she hesitated for a while and then suddenly started sobbing. She knew in that moment I was on to her and I wanted to know what was going on. After a while she opened up and started talking very fast. She told me it was her old lover who had been killed in a car accident. Years before, they had been on a road trip and the car he was driving, had been wiped out by a truck going the opposite direction. She survived with a slight leg injury, but her boyfriend was killed instantly, dying on the spot with fatal head injuries. After he died, she was inconsolable and said she could not live without him. Every night she kept calling him back until she felt his presence in her bed. She said she couldn't communicate with him, indicating she knew on some level that he hadn't crossed properly and wanted to help him as she imagined him wandering aimlessly around, totally lost and confused. Selfishly and not thinking properly, she said she wanted him to stay with her so she could look after him. She kept saying she was so happy to feel his presence again as she was lonely and she knew he followed her everywhere, never leaving her side. This was so wrong, the fact that he had never moved on and just lived in her house, a shadow of himself, sleeping and having sex with her for comfort. On so many levels she knew it wasn't right either, but was not ready to let him go.

As I pressed her for information, she said she was still having sex with her ghost boyfriend and did not think there was anything wrong with that as he always was a good lover.

Astounded, but not shocked, as I have had cases like this before, I was very careful with my words and explained to her that this was not right. He was a lost spirit and he was probably confused. I told her he did not belong in our reality and dimension. He had his own journey to do as an eternal soul and needed to cross over for his own spiritual healing, regeneration, and his soul's evolution with eternal progress. This was nothing but morally wrong, stupid, and cruel. I also said it was her personal responsibility to make this right.

Telling her to let him go, she eventually agreed, nodding her head and admitting it was becoming more difficult to keep him here. She was tired all the time because he was living off her energy and causing her to feel depressed and anxious. She also knew she was suffering from depression and the feeling of being down was starting to get to her as she had once been a very successful and active person. She then told me about all the problems in her job, how she was not coping because she felt so drained all the time, making it impossible to concentrate or make practical decisions. In fact, she knew it was wrong, agreed she was stuck in the past, and just wanted to meet someone, get married, and have lots of children.

She was very aware she had not progressed since his death, even though she had, in the past, sought grief counseling. When we headed back to the conference room, she surprised me when she suddenly stood up and told the class what had happened. When she finished her story, everyone hugged her, full of so much love and compassion. I suggested we move him on as a group. As we formed a small circle in the middle of the room, I instructed the group to use protection and all join hands. Once we did this, I showed them how to call down the light. I told the former boy-friend to open his eyes, leave, and wished him a safe and healing journey. I also told him he had loved ones waiting for him on the other side. Within seconds he was gone. When we closed down, everyone was laughing and giggling, all agreeing they did feel him leave and they could not get over the flashing lights he left in the room. By all the sparkles and bright lights there must have been a lot of angels present to assist us. I never heard from my student again, but I'll never forget how incredibly clever Spirit was to organize this incredible healing.

My Stay at a Historical Haunted Hotel

While traveling for my spirit show, I found myself staying in an incredibly haunted hotel. When I arrived in my room, I could feel a cold chill in the air and the whole place felt creepy and horrible. I kept thinking I was mad to think I was going to sleep there. As a rule, I don't like historical hotels at all, as I know they are always heavily haunted and constantly used for ghost tours. My promoter wanted me to be there, and all the tickets were sold, so I just decided to go with it. Before I was about to start my show, I nearly jumped out of my skin when I suddenly felt something icy cold touch me on the head. I had been touched several times over the years by wandering spirits, especially on my breasts, while doing shows in haunted hotels, but this really took me aback because it seemed to come out of nowhere.

Opening up psychically, I called out demanding who was there and immediately heard a loud spirit voice telling me, "Get out!"

I started burping loudly as the spirit came too close, and I could feel icy cold fingers wrapping around my neck and a deathly spirit energy creeping all over my body like a tight vine. At the same time, I could see from the corner of my eye a dark shadow hovering next to me. Everything seemed to happen so fast and, out of nowhere, I could smell a horrible, rotten spirit smell, like old mold, which began to menacingly circle around my body in rotating waves.

Yelling loudly, I called on infinite loving Spirit and the Archangel Michael to intervene and protect me. Within seconds I had the energy to gain my composure once again. Feeling my energy coming back, I called out loudly to the menacing spirit to back off while my spirit team stepped in, forcing the angry spirit into a corner of the room. Once this happened, everything slowed down and I began the dialogue again, asking who the spirit was and, more importantly, what it wanted.

The spirit said he was a soldier who had visited many years ago and that this was his room, and I was not welcome. I was not surprised by this as I had seen ghosts of soldiers walking around the building when I first showed up. Sensing the spirit was confused, I told him that he was dead, and it was time to go as his time was over on earth. No sooner had I said this, he quietly left, and the room started to feel lighter and brighter. I had a peaceful, restful sleep that night after the show and had no other issues while I stayed there.

It wasn't just me who had complained about that hotel; I had also heard complaints from students and clients about strange things going on in their rooms. One woman said she was terrified and laid awake all night. She said she felt a spirit man lying on top of her, until the morning light came into the room. I vowed not to go back there again.

The Haunted Old Theater

We have been hearing stories of hauntings and spirits in old clubs and theaters for years and yes, they do exist. Didn't they make a play about it? It was called *Phantom of the Opera*. I can imagine some of the ghostly spirits that hang around these places, as I've heard so many stories from actors and crews telling all sorts of scary tales and have experienced and seen a few myself.

One night while doing a spirit show, I walked into an old club room before the event and was taken aback by how old the run-down theater was. I also sensed it was haunted; it was incredibly cold, had a pungent stale smell, weird energy, with all the other usual haunting signs. As we began to set up the show, the feeling in my gut would not go away as I knew it was going to be a hard show. The music kept turning itself off, the microphone wouldn't work, lights kept flickering blindly in my face, and I struggled on until the intermission, furiously berating myself that I should have trusted my gut and cleared the place before starting the show. No complaints from the audience though, as energetically it was a fantastic night with heaps of really good and loving spirit connections.

As soon as the intermission came and everyone ran off for drinks, all laughing and talking among themselves and seemingly unaffected by the technical malfunctions, I walked toward the back of the stage behind the thick curtains. Suddenly a chair out of nowhere came hurdling towards me and hit me, smack right on the head. Stunned, I was taken aback and my promoter, who had been trying to fix the sound system, could not believe her eyes when she saw me lying on the floor. Once she helped me up, I commanded the spirit to come out from where it was hiding, to go into the light, and that it did not belong here and it was time to go.

When it was time for the show's second half, it must have worked because things calmed down and we had no problems with the music and microphone, making it a successful night. In fact, the energy built right up and the show ran like a dream. Curious to know who the spirit was, as I had only seen an outline of a tall shadow swoop quickly past, I told the woman who ran the place what happened and asked if she ever had problems with the room before. She said she was not surprised and moaned that the bar staff hated working there as they were always complaining about things going wrong. She said they were all convinced it was the ghost of a male entertainer who had died of a massive heart attack while working on stage.

Tracy

Tracy was a businesswoman from Queensland who moved to Sydney to set up her own consulting business. After she moved into a section of what had been an old hotel, her first year of business went well and she was successful and extremely busy. Unfortunately, over time, she started having some type of strange, paranormal activity in her office with some type of beings she could only describe as "the black ones."

At the same time, she was beginning to open up spiritually so her awareness of different types of energy was quite acute and she could pick up different energies very easily. The thing that scared her the most was fleeting black shadows, like dark wisps of putrid smoke but thicker in appearance and denser. Whenever they appeared, suddenly out of nowhere, especially near the stairs, they always left a heavy feeling in the air, like a feeling of being dirty and unwashed. Some of the other awful things she often felt was a feeling of not being able to wake up or a feeling of being pressed down by a black shadow. She also noticed, that whenever these beings appeared, they would always be accompanied by strange little mishaps or accidents, such as tripping over nothing, small cuts, dropping things, or small appliances acting up and then magically fixing themselves.

Not knowing what to do, as she had never experienced anything like this before, she just ignored it and hoped it would just go away. However, things started to get worse over time. One day, while rushing out the door to see a client at her office in the city, the energy in her home suddenly became heavy and she began to see black energy spikes from the corner of her eyes that menacingly surrounded her entire body. Feeling like she couldn't breathe, she almost screamed with fear when she felt a shove to her back between the shoulder blades. Thinking she was going to die, she started to pray out loud, imagining her body dead and bleeding, twisted in front of her. At that very same moment she couldn't believe her eyes when she saw a white being (which she believed to be an angel) appear, swoop down, and save her, wrapping her gently in its arms and placing her ever so tenderly to the ground. Not understanding what had exactly happened, she dusted herself off and rushed out the door to her meeting. The good thing was that the black ones did not appear again and seemed to disappear to wherever they came from. To this day, she is a firm believer in angels.

Hospitals, Nursing Homes, and Retirement Villages

My first experience as a young nurse was terrifying. I was only seventeen years old and very naïve. I had never experienced death or even seen a dead body, for that matter. I still remember my first experience seeing a dead person. I was so scared that I backed into a wall and nearly fainted because it looked like the body was still breathing. The patient, of course, had died, but his spirit must have been still in the room. When I opened all my psychic senses, I could hear someone talking in a low voice saying that he was soon leaving but was just waiting for his wife to see the body for the viewing. Not long after he must have crossed, because his spirit disappeared and I never saw or heard him again.

One amazing thing I witnessed working as a nurse was when a patient was dying and all their relatives in spirit would gather around. The relatives in spirit would sing songs, play piano, or talk around the bed of the dying patient. I would have a little laugh to myself when I saw spirits gathering in a room, as they can be a noisy bunch, talking to each other and always wanting to be around when someone is dying and coming home. I never told anyone about seeing those spirits gather back in those days, as I had learned at a young age that it frightens people, or they think you are raving mad. On many occasions I would be able to see a crowd of spirits playing a spirit piano, sitting on the patient's bed, or just hanging around in general. I had many patients tell me, in awe, how they saw their mother or father in spirit, standing at the end of the bed, or sitting in their room as if to comfort them in their darkest hours.

Another interesting experience was when I saw a patient die for the first time. As I sat, holding the patient's hand for support and comfort, I watched in awe as I saw, clairvoyantly, a purple energy slowly leaving the top of the patient's head—an area called the crown chakra, which is an energy point at the top of the head—and disappear into thin air, or into what I understand to be a portal into another dimension. I realize now I was witnessing the soul leaving the diseased body and returning, once again, back to the spirit world, fulfilling a cycle our spirits do time and time again.

I have also seen the souls of people who are in a coma, or unconscious, flying around the room. This can be a relief when you have sick children that are suffering and are in a coma because you know that they are not even in their bodies but flying around, free as a bird without a care in the world, watching everything below and not suffering because they are not in their bodies. As for people with dementia, people always ask where they go when not present. My answer is that I always believe they have one foot in the spirit world and one foot here while they are in their final state of that terrible disease.

Animals always know when someone is going to pass into the spirit world. You will often see a cat or a dog that lives in a nursing home, for comfort, sitting on a bed where a patient is soon passing. I have seen this happen many times and it makes you realize how incredibly psychic animals really are.

There were other spirits I experienced back in those early days of nursing. I used to call them the "lost souls." You would mainly see them at night, walking around the place as if they owned it. I hated working the nightshift and I remember the other nurses and I used to gather around at the desk and tell ghost stories all night. In hindsight it was a good thing because it kept us all awake, but we would scare ourselves silly with some of the stories we experienced. Every single nurse I have ever met has always had some type of encounter with a ghost: seeing spirit people walking around, things being moved, the lights going on and off, cold air coming out of nowhere, the elevator going up and down with nobody on it. One night, a group of us one night even saw an old nun walking around in the dead of night, who used to work at the hospital in her younger years. It was probably about three in the morning when that happened. After that incident, we never did rounds by ourselves and used to go in pairs, making sure our flashlights always shone brightly. We would often get complaints from patients, too, about strange noises or sensations, especially when they went to the toilet in the middle of the night.

In my view and experience, most of the hospitals and nursing homes I have worked in are full of spirits. Without a doubt they are a busy place for spirits to gather, just like shopping centers, airports, funeral homes, clubs, railway stations, and football stadiums just to name a few. I have even had clients that have had spirits hitch a ride in their car after they have been to the cemetery. I knew an ambulance driver who complained that someone or something kept tapping him on the shoulder every time he drove the ambulance. He kept saying he felt it was a football player he picked up that was in a car accident and had died during the ambulance drive. Sick of being tapped all the time, he said one day he lost his temper and told the spirit to get lost and go to the other side. It must have worked, as the tapping soon stopped and he was never bothered again.

Teddy

Every time Teddy, a student of mine, visited his father in a nursing home, before he died, he would always ring me up saying he had an unwelcomed spirit visitor in his home or car and would ask me to clear it. He knew these types of wandering spirits were not dangerous, but Teddy became tired of the constant problems and lack of sleep. Once these spirits moved into their "new home,"— Teddy's home— they would become a nuisance and let themselves be known by walking up and down his corridor all night, moving things around or making constant noise. One time, after we removed a spirit from his car, the strange banging noise in the back of his car suddenly stopped. After I had cleared that one, the look on Teddy's face was priceless.

Susie

One day I received a phone call from a woman called Susie who worked as a locum doctor in a retirement village. She was referred to me by her cousin whose house I had cleared a few months earlier, and so she was aware of the downsides of hauntings and spiritual interference in the home and workplace. When I spoke to her on the phone, she seemed extremely agitated, was crying, and kept repeating that she was desperate for help. She also mentioned that she had spoken to her cousin who reassured her I was perfect for the job, and I wasn't some nut case that would make her feel like she was going mad. According to the woman, something sinister seemed to be following her and was now living in her new flat. She was convinced she had picked it up from the retirement village she was working at, as it was common to have deaths in a place where many of the residents were old and sick.

The woman had only been living in the property for under a month but was convinced she wasn't alone as something or someone invisible kept lying on top of her and scaring the living daylights out of her. Crying, she said she would wake up screaming and shaking with fear in the middle of the night and as soon as she switched on the light nothing was there, except a weird smell that seemed to linger in the home no matter how much she cleaned. Things worsened when she felt a thick, dark cloud over her one night, after a week of stress because of her workload. While sleeping, she began to feel as if she couldn't breathe, then saw a black shadow reach out, grab her leg and pull her out of the bed, throwing her on the floor. Shaken, crying, and finding herself lying on the floor, she quickly got up and turned the light on but found no evidence of anyone being there.

Susie told me she was "sensitive" and could feel spirit presence in rooms ever since she was young. Deciding not to do anything about it, she threw herself into study and worked very hard. Her cousin told her to smoke the house out with some sage, as I always suggest to clients beforehand. However, the unwanted spirit was very stubborn and for some reason had a type of attachment to her because it came back a week later. Even her poor cat was affected; it was out of sorts, stopped eating, and kept snarling at nothing or the air all the time. The other strange thing that occurred was articles of clothing and underwear disappearing and reappearing in odd places. It was all very frustrating and was beginning, in Sally's words, to get really scary.

It seemed obvious to me, from what she described, that she had inherited a resident poltergeist. It sounded like it was behaving badly and trying to scare her out of her wits or trying in every way possible to get her utmost attention. Whatever this spirit was, after I did a remote viewing, I could not positively identify it, so I decided to get myself over there as fast as possible.

As I pulled up in my car at her address, I called in my spirit team and was more than curious to find out exactly what was going on in the terrified woman's home. I had worked on many cases like this before and I wasn't surprised when I started burping repeatedly outside her front door, as the energy was incredibly strong. I started to feel the usual sickness I get in my stomach when I can sense earthbound spirits are around. This happens all the time and is just part of the process. I don't need any machines because parts of my body unwittingly act as a barometer for what I call "stuck energy." I can also feel dark energy in the ground with my legs, which can often become ice cold. This sometimes becomes a pain, though, when I must explain to a client that I am not feeling sick, it is just my energy center going off like a psychic horn, as it acts like a warning or radar system when lost spirits are around. This seems to help clients relax as humor is always very comforting and healing.

No sooner had I begun walking down the long corridor of the very neat flat than I could immediately sense cold static electricity in the air. It was thick and began to surround and weave its way around my entire body like a large snake. I hesitated and sneezed for a few minutes as the energy was now hitting my nose and I could taste cold ectoplasm in my mouth. The dense spirit energy seemed mainly to be coming from the bedroom. Taking a deep breath, I stopped suddenly in my tracks when I sensed tremendous waves of thick, wild, negative energy, full of sadness, grief and desolation. It was like I was walking into a wall of utter despair. Calling out to ask who was there, I heard a male voice call back, telling me, with expletives, to get out and that I had no business being there. Then, right in front of my eyes, I saw an apparition, a ghostly figure of an outline of a young man. He appeared quite small, thin, no older than twenty, dressed in bike gear and carrying a motorbike helmet in his arms. When I asked him why he was in this flat, he said he lived there with his girlfriend. He said he vaguely remembered being hit by a truck and then coming back home because he could not find his motor bike. As I relayed the message back to Sally, she just nodded and begged me to get rid of it at once, as she was done and scared out of her wits. He then started saying how he fancied Susie and kept thinking she was his girlfriend. I told him he was dead and that he needed to cross over, as there were loved ones waiting to help him on the other side. Without any further delay, I brought down a light and commanded him to leave. Within seconds he quickly disappeared, along with the darkness and chaos surrounding him.

Jails

I have met many people that have worked in jails and have heard many stories. Most of them are the same: some weird thing going on of a paranormal nature. Jails tend to be a place where lots of people die: inmates die there, occasional suicides. Jails, for obvious reasons, have a collection of all types of negative energies. Some common complaints of paranormal activity include doors opening and closing for no reason, lights flashing on and off, and the sound of heavy footsteps in corridors while people are sleeping. Ghostly sightings in jails are well documented. Often former old jails have tours by paranormal investigators in places all around the world. You can just imagine the awful energy these places hold, with all the horror, torment, torture, and experiences behind prison walls. There is no wonder why many jails are said to be extremely haunted by former inmates, with reports of bad dreams, unexplained wails, and horrible energies affecting the people living or working in them.

Don

Don was having problems of a supernatural nature in his home. After he told me he worked in jails, I was not surprised. When I arrived at his house, we chatted as I scanned the home. Don said he had worked in the jails for years after he had changed his job from driving an ambulance because of his habit of bringing dead spirit's home. The problem was that there were just as many earthbound spirits in the jails, so he still had the same problem. Jails are full of negative energy, and murders and deaths a common occurrence in prisons, so it was no wonder over time Don had earthbound spirits following him home.

Don was a sensitive man, probably a natural medium but not practicing. He sighed when he told me about lost spirits, which had been a problem for him throughout his life. Don was very grateful when I explained there was nothing wrong with him, but it was a matter of learning how to deal with lost souls. He had learned how to smoke out a few, but they somehow kept coming back and keeping him awake at night. Some nights, his younger son was too scared to sleep in his room as he felt something jumping on him, as if to get his attention.

This time, Don needed extra help from me. The house was ice cold from all the spirits there. It took a good hour and a half before

I was able to release about a half dozen spirits from the home. It was an exhausting job, but the home felt really good after I gave it a good smoke out and opened all the windows to let all the negative energy leave. Immediately after this clearing, both Don and his wife said it felt like the home was so much lighter. The next day Don rang and said his wife wanted to thank me because it was the best night's sleep the family had in a long time. He then reassured me he would give his home a smoke out the minute he felt he might have picked up another spirit and would use a protection exercise for himself that I showed him how to do.

Bridges

I have heard many stories and helped with several haunted bridges throughout the years, with people jumping off, accidents, and other problems. The particular story I am sharing in relation to bridges is a personal one of a good friend.

Billy

One day, while drinking a coffee after doing all my shopping, I started to think of my old friend Billy for no apparent reason. We had lost track of each other over the years, and I had heard through the grapevine he had killed himself. It was so strange suddenly thinking of him, but I smiled to myself when I thought of all the fun memories we once shared and had together in our younger years. Back in the day, Billy was a Romeo—a real legend, a very sexy guy who always had you hysterically laughing, no matter what the occasion. He was a real character, a comic, who always wore tight leather pants, buckled boots and carried on with a whole entourage of glamorous women fighting for his attention. Billy loved all the attention and drama that constantly went on in his life. After a while I stopped giving him lifts as we went our separate ways when I finished my college studies. I was also glad to be out of his life, as I couldn't handle all his full-on addictions and the unfounded jealousy from his women.

After that first day of randomly thinking of Billy, I was walking through a car park with all my groceries when I got the shock of my life. I saw the very vivid outline of a strange man sitting in the passenger's seat of my car. The car was parked a short distance away and I couldn't quite see the man's face. I pressed the key for the car to open but nothing happened. I kept thinking over and over in my head, why wasn't my key working as it always did and who was the strange man sitting in my car and waiting for me? Not knowing what to do, I totally freaked out and rushed off with my shopping trolley to see if I could find somebody to help. The weird thing was the car park, which had been full, was now suddenly empty. There was not a single person to be found.

Not knowing what to do, I wheeled my trolly back hysterically and decided I would confront the intruder and tell him where to go. The trouble was, when I finally got back to the car, it was empty. The strange man sitting inside had disappeared without a trace, the car was still locked and nothing had been damaged or touched. It was as if nothing had happened at all. Confused and feeling stupid, I quickly clicked my key again. This time the boot opened, and the lights came on. Thinking I was imagining everything, I quickly packed the shopping in the boot, jumped in the driver's seat and headed off to my first destination of work for the day, still very confused and puzzled.

Everything was back to normal again until I hit the harbor bridge. As soon as I got into the outer lane, I found myself in a torrential rainstorm that came out of nowhere. Slowing the car down, I could see from the corner my eye an outline of the strange man again sitting in the seat next to me. Nearly crashing the car, I slowly turned my head to get a better look and was shocked when I saw, plain as day, my good but deceased friend Billy. He looked exactly the same as he did back in our twenties, in his tiny jeans, but he kept staring ahead and didn't say anything. I then realized it was the same spot on the bridge where he had killed himself by jumping off so many years ago. In that moment, I heard my guide tell me that Billy needed my help. Opening my psychic abilities and saying a quick prayer of protection, I tuned in to Billy's energy, with tears running down my face and tried to make contact. It did not take long to realize he was totally confused and did not really understand what I was talking about. It was then I realized he was lost and probably hadn't crossed over. The whole thing made me feel really sad as I kept thinking he must have been wandering aimlessly around for years with no one to help him. As soon as I drove off the bridge, I was able to stop the car and finally send him off properly. With tears running down my face, I told him he was loved, but he was dead. It was time to open his eyes, to see the light and go. I also said his mother, who had died after him, was on the other side and probably waiting for him with loving arms. He would probably get into trouble with her, but it would be okay.

Within seconds, he disappeared right in front of my eyes. Everything was back to normal again. The rain had stopped, the sun was shining, and wiping my eyes and taking a big breath, I started the car again. When I got home, I lit a candle for Billy, told him I missed him, would love him always, and finally said, after choking back tears, I was so happy he was finally safe and not to worry. I told him he would receive so much healing now that he had finally arrived back in the spirit world.

Antiques

In my experience, it is common to have negative energy due to lost souls and spirits hanging around antiques as well. It's important to always smoke cleanse an antique item before you take it into your home. A lost soul will form an attachment of some type and you can often see them hanging around the object of their desire, upsetting the natural chi in your space. I also hear stories from people all the time inheriting antiques or buying them, only to find, once they have brought the item into the home, that it causes negative energy shifts. Some people also complain of having bad luck or suffer from a fear that they have been cursed. This is the same for gifts, or items you have collected from past toxic relationships that bring you bad luck. Through the energy of the item, the person can psychically attack you. I had a client once who kept all her valuable jewelry from a toxic relationship under her bed, only to feel the former partner's energy while trying to sleep. She was never able to feel free of him until I told her to cut the energetic cords and ties with him and smoke cleanse all her jewelry. Once she did this, she never had problems sleeping again and was able to live a happy life.

John

Years ago, my husband and I lived next door to an older gentleman, John, who loved to collect antiques. He had so many of what he called his "priceless beauties" that his place actually looked, grotesque, like the home in *The Addams Family*. As soon as you stepped into the house, you could see he had antiques stuffed in every nook and cranny. I could not help but wonder if he was an expensive hoarder and perhaps suffered from loneliness after living so many years by himself after his mother's death.

His home always had an eerie feeling: it was freezing cold in the middle of summer and quite often I saw lost souls and visiting spirits walking around the place and standing next to some of the big pieces he talked about and collected. One of these lost souls was his mother, as I recognized her from a picture on his mantel piece. He quite often talked about her and on special occasions you could smell a distinctive strong perfume, wafting through the house. It didn't surprise me that John had inherited her house after living together for years.

When John died from a cruel illness, I found his spirit in my garage a couple of weeks after his funeral. He was making a loud noise and standing next to a painting he had given us before he died. I was not surprised that he had come back for the painting, as his relatives who got everything in the will and never visited him when he was alive, sold off all his beautiful antiques and refused to bury him with his cherished urn as he requested. He seemed confused and it was not possible to talk to him, so I gently explained to him he was dead, it was time to cross, and that his mother and loved ones were waiting for him on the other side. I also assured him, with tears in my eyes, he would no longer be lonely again. It made me realize how the spirit of the person can attach to items they loved when they die. It is no wonder antiques will sometimes carry a certain energy—good or bad—from the person who owned it. Whenever I see antiques in homes, I will always tell the owner to give it a good smoke cleanse to move the spirit on. Over the years, I have crossed many spirits found clinging to their possessions.

The Haunted Marionette Puppet

While traveling around in Europe with my husband many years ago, I bought a marionette puppet at a marketplace. It was unique, so very charming, and dressed like a jester or clown. It had funny eyes, but I was drawn to it and kept going back thinking I needed to buy it as a gift for my daughter.

When I brought it home, my daughter complained she didn't like it. She said it was creepy and that it watched her all the time. One night she said she thought she saw its shadow bobbing up and down, as if it had come to life. She said it was haunted, and, thinking it was rubbish because I thought the puppet was so cute, I gave it to my mother, who said she loved it. Not long after, my mum changed her mind and rang me to tell me to get rid of the puppet. She said it was evil, nobody liked it, and she had banished it to my old bedroom. When I came to get it, I felt sorry for the puppet. However, as I tuned in to its energy, I could sense a spirit had attached itself to it, probably its previous owner, who was dead. After clearing the spirit and finally smoking the puppet, I saw some type of gray, darkish energy leave. Instead of throwing it in the bin after seeing the negative energy leave, I gave it a new home where it would be appreciated and loved.

CHAPTER 4

TYPES OF ENERGIES

Everything is made of energy and has its own unique vibration, which includes you and everyone around you. We are constantly in a state of radiating and receiving energy. The frequency of this energy is on a spectrum from light to dark. Light energy is warm, fun, loving, contagious, and light. Dark energy, or shadow energy, which is rooted in fear, is heavy, dense, sometimes sticky, can move fast, but it doesn't last long. Dark energy blocks our evolution to raise to higher levels of our own spirituality and reality. As electro-magnetic beings, we attract experiences and relationships matched to our frequency. For example, if you have low self-esteem and do not love yourself, you will always attract the same situations in your life until you have done healing on yourself. It is important to release pain, fear, and hatred you may be carrying from your childhood or past lives, and use a good therapist to do so. Unless you take personal responsibility, nothing will change.

People will often ask me how to recognize different energies to understand how to be wary of certain types of people and spirits. Sometimes this is difficult to recognize. All I can say is to always trust your gut, intuition or feelings—they are never wrong. For spirits, it's the same. Just because they are dead does not mean they are suddenly "holier than thou." Most lost souls are confused, but there are a few that can be very manipulative and dark, causing all types of havoc in your life if you don't clear them. I treat them as I would any spirit because they do have an intelligence.

Dark Soul Energy

Living dark soul energy souls generally stay dark after they have died, and are of a lower vibration than those of us with lighter energies; I am sure you have met a few. These souls are negative. They may be found in your own family, church, or social groups. These types of souls are often attracted to having high positions in society because they are driven by ego. That does not mean all successful people are evil. Lost souls and earthbound spirits don't have to be evil, but the dark souls are always evil and malevolent. As for people that are attracted to the darker side of life, such as hurting and manipulating others for their own greed and ego, I believe they will never get far in life and end up, karmically, in the cycle of evolution, paying for their deeds at some stage and ending up having unhappy, empty lives. The same goes for people that throw curses. Karmically, the energy will always return. If you look in their aura, you will see heavy colors of black. The aura may also be shrunken, similar to how an aura may look when a person is sick or depressed. Dark souls do not tolerate light energies because they are incompatible with their frequencies and will often clash. Over time these energies will learn it is impossible to co-exist, no matter how hard these energies try.

Light Soul Energy

Lighter energy people, angelic energy beings, are here to help mankind and to progress, karmically, to higher levels in the spirit world and in soul groups. They are here on earth for a higher purpose, usually to help and assist mankind for their soul's purpose. Light souls repel the energy of darker souls, so quite often the dark soul will move on if a light soul is around. Light souls have amazing energy fields or auras. The colors are very clear and you will see streaks of gold and silver with other vibrant, warm colors.

The more time you work on yourself, the higher your vibration will be and the brighter your light will shine. The ability to forgive people for their wrong doings is actually setting your own soul free. I believe that good deeds often come back and offer a sense of future happiness, as in the Law of Attraction. They create a sense of community here on earth, a feeling of togetherness and an obligation of mutual responsibility, respect, and unconditional love toward others, while completing their spiritual contracts here on earth. They also get a "helper's high," which is produced by the brain releasing endorphins, the feel-good chemicals of the brain, the same ones you get from exercise. When people do good things for you, you get a feeling of great satisfaction and gratitude.

Have you ever noticed how some people just shine when they walk into a room? If you want to raise your energy, tell more people you love them and learn how to forgive. Begin with yourself: take personal responsibility for your own actions, move on from toxic people and situations, be mindful of your thoughts and actions, and use every aspect of kindness in your life. It also helps to be grateful for what you have, be happy for others, reserve jugments, care for the earth, and to generally believe in your dreams for a better world.

Gray Soul Energy

For years people have asked me what a gray soul is. This energy can be seen in people who waver between light and dark. I call these weakened souls, as they often lose their way and have no purpose. I have had experience with this type of energy from students and friends whose intentions initially were good but ended up falling into a power struggle from ego and jealousy. Similar to a dark soul, the aura of a gray soul appears shrunken and weak. Blotches of dark and gray energy are evident in the aura.

Over time you will learn all the types of different energies, especially if you are opening up to develop yourself for valuable insights. To open yourself to identifying types of energies, it is best to first start with practicing meditation to raise your own energy levels. It's easy to do once you learn how. You just have to make the time. It helps with your general attitude of trusting that things will always work out for you no matter the odds, to be patient with outcomes, be positive, stop stressing on the negative, go with the flow, and to always live in the now. This way you are more focused.

Finally, the gift of prayer is remarkable and will always work. Don't forget to use prayer every day, as it creates miracles not only for yourself but others who are sick or not doing so well. By definition, a miracle is an action that runs counter to the commonly observed processes of nature. With practice and an open mind and heart, the pathway of discovery is always open for the student who works with unconditional love and quality and energy of Spirit.

Always trust your gut when recognizing good and negative energies. You will always know what's right and wrong for you, no matter what you tell yourself. Second guessing is a waste of time and a load of rubbish. Intuition is your own innate gift from Spirit you were given at birth from heaven. Therefore, own and acknowledge your inner wisdom, as we all have a degree of psychic abilities. The more you own your intuition—that golden radar of pure intelligence, detection and knowing—the more confident you will feel on your life's journey. Once you intentionally accept this wisdom, life will be easier.

Negative Energy

Negative energy is very common and is generally left over from the last people that have lived in a property or worked there. It seems to ingrain itself into the whole energy of a physical structure and does not go away unless it is smoked out, sometimes taking several cleansings. Negative energy may also come with bad smells, reminiscent of dirty socks and shoes or moldy clothes. You may also feel as if you have a black cloud over your head or sudden depression.

It is possible to get negative energy from people when they visit, including family members. Often people will drain your energy with their bad moods, mind games, constant problems, rudeness, or any kind of interference to your general well-being. Many people can experience this with bad family members, while buying a house, or unpleasant visitors. These types of energy-drainers can leave you feeling flat and tired after a visit. It's similar to the vibe or bad feeling you pick up when you first meet someone. First impressions are always correct; always trust your gut. It's never wrong. If more people did this, there would be fewer problems in the world. I always recommend people give their new home a good smoke cleansing when they first move in because negative energies like to linger.

Larry

One day I received a phone call from a client, a businessman I had met at a conference who had just bought a place in Sydney's eastern suburbs. Larry was a hard-working man in his early fifties who had just relocated from the United States. He had his own company, traveled a lot, and was looking forward to living in the home he had just purchased. He was married to a wonderful woman and they had two children. However, once they moved into the home, they were all constantly fighting, and everything seemed to be going wrong.

When I arrived at Larry's, he welcomed me warmly, but from the moment I stepped onto the property my alarm bells began to ring. I did not get a good feeling. The house, though very grand on the outside, felt lonely, creepy, and sad; it was full of negative energy that hit you right in the gut. It did not feel welcoming at all, and I shuddered and crossed my arms to protect myself when I felt the coldness emanating from the property slip into my consciousness.

As soon as I stepped through the front door and into the hallway, the sadness I was sensing became overwhelming and seemed to follow me like a menacing shadow. It did not take me long to work out the problem because as soon as I stepped into the master bedroom, the energy became thick, dense, and extremely depressing. Scanning the room, I could sense there were definitely no earthbound spirits in the home, but there was a lot of dark, negative energy, especially in the spot where Larry and his wife slept. Without saying much, I silently opened myself up. Then I began to psychically pick up the sounds of screaming and yelling coming from implanted memories in the home's walls.

When I told Larry what I had heard, he looked at me dumbfounded for a while. Then he admitted that I was correct, as the couple he had bought the house from, as far as he could work out, must have been always fighting. Larry told me the man had been nearly impossible to make a deal with and his wife was always yelling in the background whenever Larry's solicitor had spoken to them on the phone. When it came time for them to sign, the man was aggressive and unpleasant to deal with. My intuition told me this problem was most certainly left behind by the previous owners. The energy we were experiencing was their negative residue.

I have seen this time and time again, and I always encourage people to clear the energy in their new homes as soon as they move in, so not to be affected by the energy of the former residents. The most effective way of doing this is by doing a smoke cleansing. Larry must have picked up on my thoughts because, without me having to say a word, he began to blurt out all the problems he was having since his family moved in. He complained that he and his wife kept arguing and could not agree on anything. In the meantime, she had returned to the States to visit her sick mother and had taken the children with her. Before she had left, she had moved into another bedroom on the far side of the house and they had not been speaking. He was heartbroken and did not know what to do to fix the relationship.

Standing in Larry's bedroom, I got to work straight away and brought down a white light and wrapped it around myself for protection. As soon as I did this, I could sense the full impact of the dark energy in the room. It felt sad, lonely, and extremely cold. Saying a prayer, I brought down a beacon of pure, loving light and, in my mind, made a portal in the ceiling of the room and pushed the negative energy out into the yard and buried in it the ground. Once this was done, I flooded the room with healing light then closed the vortex of energy and finished the clearing with a smoke cleansing to make sure the negative residue was gone, out through the open windows. Evil, dark or thick black energy will often be impossible to send into white loving energy, so it is best grounded back into the earth for the nature spirits to heal. Before too long, the home's energy felt clear and back in balance again.

When I had finished, I started one more smoke cleansing and smoked the whole room out. I wafted smoke inside cupboards and wardrobes where negative energy might have been trapped or hiding. When I had finished cleansing the room, I placed the bowl of the smoking herbs very carefully in the middle of the bed so it could gently keep burning until the energy in the room was completely clear. Somehow, the glass bowl exploded and burst into flames, the embers landing on the sheets and blankets on the bed. Screaming, we quickly opened the windows and grabbed the burning bedding and threw it outside, where it landed on the lawn below. Then we both ran outside and grabbed the hose and put out the fire that, unbelievably, continued to burn. In all my years of clearing houses and offices and working with sage, I have only twice experienced anything like that before. Not knowing what to say, we both looked at each other and started to laugh. Larry may have lost some sheets and blankets that day, but his wife came back almost straight away. I continue to receive Christmas cards from the family thanking me and sharing how happy they are.

Interference Energy

Over time, homes can have interference energy, which I describe as feeling like a small tornado vortex. This type of energy can create a spiritual opening to another dimension. I like to compare it to the human aura. A vortex is best described as a whirlwind of moving matter in the shape of a spiral (sometimes described as tornadoes) that can be suppressed, plugged and stopped. As I have said, a vortex, if left open, can work as an open door or portal to another dimension to unwelcomed guests or spirits from the astral world. This can be easily dealt with by closing down the vortex and visualising and sending white light into the open vortex. By simply rubbing your hand chakras together and sending healing energy into the problem you can close the vortex down.

An open vortex, when first scanned psychically, will feel like a subtle, cold gentle breeze to the hands. Once closed down, the space will be restored to its natural balance and chi energy. This type of energy or problem can be caused by negative energy from abusive people with their actions and emotions, like domestic violence, or continued drug use, witchcraft, or continual abuse of Ouija boards, as these situations often leave psychic imprints in the space. Vortices can also be caused by lost souls that have disrupted the energy of the home and have congregated there for a period of time. These problems are often found in hallways or near bathrooms and laundries. They are easy to locate, heal, and close down once you have located them.

How to Close It Down

Once you have removed all the lost souls, look for the affected area by running your hands along the ceiling till you feel a cool breeze. You could also use a pendulum, which will swing side by side when the interference energy is detected. Once you find the affected area, rub your hands together and send white light energy into the area. I do this by placing my hands over the area, which may be in the corner of a room near the ground or high on a ceiling, then visualizing white light going in to the vortex. Once this is completed, I will often feel a *pop* sound in my ear. I then know the area is now safe and closed down. I have run across vortices quite a lot in places I have worked, especially when there have been lost souls around for a long time, causing disruption to the energy of a space. I always look for vortices in the breaks in the structures of buildings. When you think about it, it is like scanning the energy field of a person. Often when people are sick or have been through some traumatic event, they will often have little tears in their auras which can lead to attachments and exposure from outside influences, making them feel oversensitive. I learned this from my early days as a spiritual healer.

The Difference Between a Portal and a Vortex

A portal is an entry point, bridge, doorway or gateway between two locations, or dimensions. They can be a conduit for dark and negative energies and entities. Once opened, they can be a conduit for new and positive light frequencies. We can open and close them to get rid of negative energies or entities that don't belong in a dimension. We aim to open portals to evolutionary energies and close them to the dark areas of the astral plane.

A vortex is best described as a whirlwind of moving matter in the shape of a spiral. The earth has many vortices in many sacred spaces like Sedona and Uluru where ley lines, or energy lines, cross. It is said that natural vortices can provide us the ability to travel energetically between dimensions. This is why it is common to feel like you are going out of your body, feel sleepy, or even the opposite— feel energized—when you are around vortices. They tend to exist where there are strong concentrations of gravitational anomalies.

Sharna

My experience with a vortex happened when I was helping a friend, Sharna, with some energy cleansing. Sharna's home was a real workout for me, as it had taken longer than I had anticipated. I was so happy I had called in an assistant to help for the day. I was fully protected, but my energy was starting to weaken, so I reached for a sweet to pick me up. After working on her property for about forty minutes and feeling as if we were being watched by prying invisible eyes, both spirit and human, I finished scanning the house psychically. Not surprisingly I discovered a vortex, which was creating a large portal or large dimensional tear or inter-dimensional opening, in one of the bedrooms. This vortex was the main cause of most of the problems in the home. There were too many lost spirits in such a small area. The energy in the room was freezing and the portal was, to my understanding, creating havoc as spirits came and went as they pleased. This was affecting the balance and harmony of the home both upstairs and downstairs. As soon as I told Sharna this information, she agreed that this was indeed the spot in the house where most of the spirit visitations were taking place and where she felt she was having the most problems at night.

Other energy workers had cleared the unwanted spirits before, but they had not checked for tears or energetic breaks on the property. The portal, I explained, was a problem and had to be closed down so the home could heal. It was creating chaos and, more importantly, allowing unwanted spirits to come and go as they pleased. No sooner had we repaired the dimensional tear with white light and closed down the leaking energy, my ears began to ache painfully and to buzz loudly. Within seconds, two spirits appeared in the room and stood by me and Sharna. One appeared as an old man and the other was a female energy, probably his wife. The female spirit seemed scared, but the male energy was extremely fierce and angry. Suddenly the whole room changed in temperature, and I could feel "prickly energy" like electricity, in the air, making all my hairs stand up on my arms. Stepping forward, I asked who the spirits were and what they wanted. The male told me his name and how he and his wife had lived in the house for as long as they could remember. He asked what we were doing there, and it was obvious that he had no idea that he was dead. He remembered being sick and dying there but nothing else. The male spirit also wanted to know who the noisy people living in his house were and about the screaming man who lived upstairs.

Before I could answer, I was pushed across the room and landed on the bed on the opposite side of the room. As soon as this happened, my assistant stepped forward, and, without wasting any time, brought down the white light. As soon as this was done, we held hands, said our usual prayer, several times in fact and proceeded to talk to the spirits gently, telling them that they were dead and to open their eyes and to go into the light so they could cross over and go home. Within a few moments, we felt them leave and the temperature in the room change. All that was left were little gray dots that eventually disappeared too. The healing had taken place and their own guides had come and helped them cross over. Once the couple entered the light, I heard a big thank you and goodbye and knew that everything would be all right. This made me leave a mental note to myself to always ask somebody to assist when doing big homes or properties.

How to Close Portholes or Open Vortexes

Begin this exercise by closing your eyes and taking three deep breaths, in through your nose and out through your mouth. As you do this, wrap some white light around your whole body for protection and imagine opening all your chakras, or energy centers. If you want to, you can choose a little prayer as well. Something that you may have remembered as a child. Some people may prefer to work with an angel, or whatever higher being you are called to, while others like to use protective crystals and use the devas within them.

Once you feel grounded and centered, starting from the front door of a property, rub your palms together, which opens the chi energy up from your hand chakras, then place them upwards while you scan the ceilings and structure of the property.

As you do this, walk slowly room by room, starting from the front door, scan the energy with your hands until you feel a little draft or breeze on your hands. Some people like to use a dowser wand or stick, but I feel your hands are the best indicators, as I always believe the body is a good barometer of what is going on around you when it comes to energy. Don't forget to use all your senses as they are valuable tools and easy to use when you practice.

As soon as you feel a subtle breeze or feel cold on your hands, you will know you have an energetic break and need to close it down, as it may be used for other lost spirits or souls to just drop in.

You open the energy centers in your hands by rubbing your hands together, which will activate your hand chakras that are located in the middle of your palms. Once you have done this, imagine a white light and run it down through your body to your heart then your hand chakras. Allow the energy to flow through both your hands toward the area you are working with for a minute or two, or until you no longer feel any breeze. When you have finished sending energy, shake your hands.

Once you have finished, imagine closing down your chakras like little lights, wash white light through your body and finally, wash your hands, giving them a good scrub, as negative energy can stick.

Residual Energy or Psychic Imprint

Residual energy, or what I like to call a psychic imprint, is what is left behind after an emotionally-charged event—good or bad. An example could be war, a fierce battle, suffering, death, murder, mental or physical abuse and torture, all of which could create a negative imprint. You can also have a positive imprint created by weddings, religious ceremonies, party or a family gathering. I believe the earth is like a huge magnetic tape recorder recording everything that happens and leaving an imprint on the material world. Some people can tune in to these imprints and experience it for themselves. The person may feel fear, sickness, their energy drained, frightened, anxious or even occasionally happy.

This is often found on ghost tours where you can experience the dark side and haunted history of old places and buildings. Generally, everyone will feel the energy and even sense spirits around them while guided by historians and engaging story guides and investigators. There are literally thousands of paranormal hotspots all around the world where they get large crowds of curious and adventurous people there for a thrill. If you never believed in ghosts, it will all be changed in a matter of time once you have embarked on your tour

If you have residual energy in your home or place of work, it has a history and is old. You will know right away, as you will feel the energy is not right or not how it should normally be because it will feel cold and sickening. Your hairs may even stand on end.

The residual energy can only be described as giving you a sickening feeling in your stomach, as if you want to vomit. The energy may also have a smell, which may take a couple of days to go away, depending on the severity of the case and the number of spirits rescued and removed. I always recommend to throw caution to the wind with my clients and to make sure they wrap themselves in the white light before going to a place that is haunted, or a ghost tour, as this type of energy can be intimidating.

I also suggest a little prayer for protection if they are sensitive souls or open to energies. Also make sure you are working with a professional tour operator who has experience, is highly qualified and understands energies. I personally don't like these tours as I am too sensitive. I often feel the dread in the air and on more than one occasion, I have had unwanted spirits follow me home, jumping in the back of my car and playing with my GPS, taking me all over the city. If you feel as if you have tapped into something unpleasant or picked up some creepy energy that feels upsetting, don't keep it a secret. Tell someone or do something, such as giving yourself a good ssmoke cleansing.

You need to use common sense with this and to trust your own intuition and judgment. As soon as you feel things are not right, give your home or space a good smoke cleansing for negative energy. I would also suggest a salt bath and smoke cleanse for yourself to wash off any negative energy you may have picked up. It may be helpful to call a spiritual healer or medium to help you.

The Old Theater

One of the creepiest hauntings happened when I visited a haunted theater, which was run by two paranormal investigators I knew that had been working for a longtime doing tours. They were hosting a book launch at the old theater, a haunted venue I had never been before. When it was my turn to get up on the stage as a guest speaker, I found it impossible to say anything audible except for a few grunts. I got the feeling the old theater was haunted from the chill in the air, the old seats opening and slamming shut, and a feeling of fingers touching my head.

My mouth completely dried out, as if a mischievous spirit had completely drained it of all fluids. As soon as I stepped onto the stage, the old theater lights blinded me, rendering me off-balance and making me feel blind. Feeling out of my depth, I started shaking uncontrollably and felt woozy in the head and like I was going to spin out, which is not normal for me as a seasoned professional hosting many of my own spirit shows. This had never happened before. The funniest thing was when I kept asking for a drink of water, I heard a spirit voice say, "Don't drink the water. It's dirty."

Meanwhile, blinded by the old theater lights, I managed to pull in my own spirit team for assistance. Gradually, my body began to relax and my mouth did not feel so dry.

Looking back, I had a good laugh about the events of that night and was angry with myself I forgot to use protection, even though I preach about it all the time. I should have realized that weird things were taking place from the moment I walked in. I do rescue work and am a trance channel, and the spirits in the place were probably waiting to have a go at me, as I am sure whatever spirits were there had no intention of going anywhere. When I told the paranormal investigators what had happened, they were amused and said it was the ghost of old George, the star of their show, who was a chronic alcoholic and obvious larrikin in his days. Finally jumping in the car, I took off as fast as I could and realized my GPS wasn't working—I was being directed all over the place due to two spirits in the back of the car, which I finally sent off.

Ghost tours are not for me, but they confirm that lost souls do exist.

The Astral World

The astral world is an in-between world, cold, gray and unchattered with many types of low vibrational energies, entities and lost spirits traveling throughout it. From my near-death experience in my early twenties, it was nothing like the spirit world, which is unconditional pure love. From my teenage astral traveling days, I saw lots of weird things and not everything was "love and light." I always felt safe traveling in the astral world, as I knew I'd always been pulled back to our world by the spiritual silver cord attached to my body. The silver chord in metaphysical studies refers to a life linkage from the higher self down to the physical body.

One client who needed my help with spirit rescue thought he was an expert with EVP when he went on a ghost tour in a bus with a paranormal investigator. Instead of being an observer, he thought himself to be an expert and took matters into his own hands, which is dangerous and distressful to the paranormal investigator and to himself and any inhabitants in his home. I found this out when I went to his house as a follow-up to an initial clearing I did there, as he complained there was still activity and I hadn't done my job.

When I arrived, I was surprised I had missed a lingering spirit that was sitting on the lounge. Lucky for me, his girlfriend confessed that this client was continually communicating with the dead and often did EVP with her and his friends all the time. After I cleared the confused spirit, I told him the client he was a pest and not to contact me again.

CHAPTER 5

PROTECTION METHODS

To do any type of spiritual work takes time, dedication, patience, and persistence, as you are always learning. As you undertake spiritual work, you must always use protection and study it as an important part and tool of the work. Anyone that does not do this is taking a risk as the work often takes place in other dimensions with sometimes dark, negative, confused, or trickster souls.

One of the first things I learned on my spiritual journey as an energy worker is the importance of protection. As an empath and sensitive soul, I would not be able to survive without protecting myself every day in the world, starting the moment I wake up in the early morning and open my eyes for the new day. I believe everyone should practice protection methods, especially when working with lost souls and energies that are not tangible.

I learned to do this as a young girl to stop the constant traffic from the many visiting spirits that would wake me up to get my attention. Sometimes in the bedroom I shared with my sister when I was a child, it would feel like a busy railway station, with spirits walking all over the place. I would have many sleepless nights under a hot and uncomfortable sheet, trying to find some kind of protection from all these spirits. Eventually I learned to leave a light on and use spiritual protection. This protection took the form of a white loving bubble I visualized around myself, (which is a visualization of unconditional love with all the healing colors of the rainbow), my bed, and the room. Once I created this bubble of protection, I was safe, and nothing ever happened. To this day, I still use this simple and easy technique, with the same results. I know it works and I will always feel safe, protected, and confident no matter where I am in the world.

Not everyone in the world is love and light. This is okay because not only are those beings teaching us forgiveness, but we also have free will to move away from those beings to find others that are more in alignment with our own frequencies and loving energy. Life is like a stage with so many incredible good and bad experiences. We've all been burned at some point in our lives and the lesson always is: it's time to move, and the faster you do this, the better you will be, so you don't have to do another round of heartache and disappointment. This is not only for relationships, but for toxic friends, families, and intolerable work situations. If you cannot move away, use protection as it will be very beneficial and stop negative energy from attacking your energy fields.

In my industry I have seen a lot of so-called spiritual people who are not loving and only have their own interests at heart. Spiritual teachers can come and go and are from all walks of life. The one thing I have learned is if you don't take notice of red flags in the beginning of a relationship, the more you will suffer in the end. People who work with dark energies can be very manipulative That's why it is so important to trust your gut and your intuition.

Not all lost souls are good either. They may be confused and move on quickly when you send them off, but there are others that are dark, manipulative and fight to stay. I don't know how many times I have heard clients say, "Oh I like the old ghost who lives here, don't send him or her off. It's not hurting anyone."

This is very common and so wrong as lost souls do not belong here and need to cross to finish the journey of their soul's purpose.

White Light

White light used for protection is the highest energy you can use when working with forces of a paranormal nature. There is nothing like it—it is unconditional love in its highest form. Not all spirits are good, just like people we know in our everyday lives. Just because, say someone dies and they were bad when alive, it doesn't mean they are suddenly angels or good spirits when we connect with them in the afterlife. Not all souls learn their lessons and when we go to the life view in the afterlife and look back at our spiritual contracts, it doesn't mean our souls go to a higher level.

These days I am constantly wrapping white light around myself, my family, pets and friends. I even wrap it around my car so I never have an accident. If I am out alone, I will use it for protection as wells. For added protection from psychic attack and gossip, I will also wrap a blue cloak around myself the minute I open my eyes and step out of my bed. This works really well for sensitive souls. White light visualisation and prayer is something I learned through the spiritual churches and to help me always feel safe.

Many people may have heard the term but do not know what it is. White light is the highest form of light consciousness energy, or universal love. It is powerful, loving, gentle, positive, and provides spiritual protection from negative energies when visualised and used. It is can provide healing on so many levels. White light can be used by anyone and is particularly important for empathic people to use, as it shields you from the effects of feeling the emotions of others. To use the white light is very simple, whether you are using it for protection or for healing purposes. Once you have wrapped yourself in this light, visualize a blue, silver, and gold cloack around you, as these colors are significant for energies on this planet. They also act as a deterrent to shield and stop psychic attack from other so-called light workers that work in the dark and entities that work at a lower level.

How to Work with White Light

The first thing to do is find a quiet, comfortable place to sit. Then, with your eyes closed, while you are breathing in and out slowly and deeply, say a little prayer and ask for the highest protection.

An example of this is, "I am an open channel to the universal consciousness or pure love. I am a clear and perfect channel of love, let love and light be my guide."

Or, "The light of the Holy surrounds me, the essence of all that is love, now enfolds me, the power of Almighty Spirit protects me now, The presence of pure love watches over me, Wherever I am, Almighty spirit is."

Or a simple goddess prayer is, "Blessed be the mother of the Goddess, by all her many names. May she bless my family and friends. May she bless the animals of the world and all the people everywhere."

If you are using the white light for protection, you simply ask for the white light and envision it coming down and enveloping you, so that you are in what appears to be a bubble. Once the white light is surrounding you, state your intention. For example, you could say, "Protect me from the negative energy I will encounter today." There are many different mantras and chants you can use.

Surrounding yourself in white light like this will assist in ensuring you aren't affected by those that are draining on your energy—you know who those people are!

For self-healing, however, instead of surrounding yourself in the white light you visualise the white light entering your body through the top of your head, through the crown chakra, still breathing slowly and deeply, visualise the white light as it travels to each chakra in your body. Allow it to cleanse each chakra until you feel light and visualise it moving on to the next, until finally it reaches the earth star chakra that keeps you grounded, anchored and protected by mother earth or Gaia.

White light visualisation can be used on a daily basis, helping you feel balanced, calm and positive. If the energy is toxic, I always visualize a dark blue and gold buble around me as an extra shield, something I sometimes call a pearl bubble.

I always use this exercise before any work, after work and to protect my home, car, family, pets and almost anything I am worried about or want to protect.

If I am going anywhere where I do not feel safe, as well as the white light, I wrap a blue cloak around me for extra protection. This is good to use when you are working or dealing with people that do not have your best intentions in mind and may be inclined to use psychic attack.

Boundaries

Once you are on this path, Spirit will send you all types of people, from all walks of life, which will be attracted to your energy like a magnet and who in turn will need your assistance and help in so many ways. Just remember to make sure you keep your boundaries up, your protection intact, and do not take these people on as friends. Often the people you help will drain you of all your own energy and are unwilling to help you if you are in need. I don't know how many times I have walked into a shop or place and the someone there will just come up to me and tell me all of their problems. I have also worked in the media where other so-called readers, healers, and other mediums have suddenly befriended me just so I can help them in whatever is going on in their life. Once they receive the information they need, your kindness is often never reciprocated for the fantastic so-called "swap" they were going to give you.

Psychic Attack and Staying Healthy

Psychic attack was another problem I had when I first opened up and I must have been an easy target for so many parasites out there in the astral. Meditation helped with this as it lifted my energy and increased my vibration, allowing more light into my light body until the dark forces, parasites and entities found it almost impossible to affect me in any way. Daily exercise is another good thing to do, such as yoga, walking in nature, or any type of general exercise as it keeps you strong and fit both mentally and psychically. Martial arts is excellent as it keeps your energy grounded, focused and in alignment, especially if you are very sensitive and psychic, as you are able to work for long hours and stay focused. These days there are so many things you can get into such as chakra dancing, or anything you can have fun with to stay fit and healthy. I once worked with a woman who was a very good reader until she started to drink every night because of her personal worries and emotional problems she never seemed to deal with over the years. After a while her readings became extremely negative and off the mark and it was no surprise when all her clients began to suddenly drop off like flies until she was forced to close up her business.

Another, what I can only describe as extremely ambitious woman I worked with in the media, starved herself on a daily basis so she could look a certain way. I know the camera does add a few inches to our frames, but her obsession with herself and what she looked like went way beyond the extreme. In the end, she was totally scattered and her readings never made any sense at all. Before too long she became very sick, forgot what shifts she was supposed to work and was no longer looked upon as a reliable worker. It was not too long before she was soon asked to leave and was replaced by another medium. I have always believed in healthy food, healthy mind, and healthy body. If we could just remember our body is our temple, which we need to use in this life so we need to take care of it. I believe we can perform so much better in our acquired type of work in the world and reach the top of our fields, if only we looked after ourselves.

The more you work on yourself and meditate on a daily basis, the more light you will bring into your own light body and refrain from negative excesses. That is why meditation is so important in our lives. It will also clear your channel giving you a strong energy link to the spirit world, where you will have an excess of loving information given to you on a daily basis.

Vibrational flower essences such as clematis in the Bach flowers and red lily in the Australian bush flower essences are good as well, taken on a daily dose, homoeopathically. If you feel ungrounded, a good way to clear your head is to go out in nature. Stand barefoot on the grass or soil and raise your hands above your head while breathing in and extend your fingers, slowly lowering them toward the earth while breathing out, lowering your arms toward the ground. Also, just the simple act of hugging a tree will ground you.

Ever since I started doing this work professionally, which is part of my spiritual purpose or contract, I have always meditated daily and made an effort to exercise daily. This has become an integral part of my work. This process not only keeps me strong, physically, mentally, emotionally, and spiritually, but also helps keep my channel clear and I am able to raise my vibration to a higher level and access information needed for the client. Music, catching up with friends, and entertainment are good ways to add some positivity into your life and not make your life so serious.

Meditation for Clearing the Aura

I encourage anyone that works with energy and spirit to do this easy exercise. It helps clear entities, parasitic energy, blockages, and negative energies from the aura. It is highly effective. I have learned to do this from my learning of spiritual healing. You don't have to be psychic to do this exercise; it can be used for everyone, even children, as it lifts and sweeps negative energy out of the aura. It helps if you're feeling scattered, blocked, negative, confused, or feel as though you cannot make decisions.

Find a quiet place or go to your sacred space and light a candle. Sitting up nice and straight, keeping your chakras and energy centers in alignment, slowly breathe in and out three times, each time feeling yourself relaxing, as this is your intention.

Now gently visualise yourself starting to bring healing energy up from the earth star, deep from the earth below, into your base chakra.

As you slowly do this, feel the powerful earth energy, moving slowly upwards in your body, through every chakra, or energy point in your body, releasing negative energy, or blocks with your breath. beginning with root (red), sacral (orange), solar plexus (yellow), heart (green), throat (blue), third eye (indigo), crown (purple), and transpersonal point (white).

As you do this, feel all your chakras align, like they are being tied to a bow, as you reach the transpersonal point, which is above the crown chakra at the top of the head.

Continue this process, all the while, moving slowly upwards, making sure you continue to breathe in and out, clearing your chakras as you continue to move slowly upward through all your chakras.

Now visualize yourself in a white room. As you stand there, look to the right and if you see anything standing there, tell it to go into the light, into the light, into the holy spirit. Now look to the left, do the same. If you see anything there, or a dark color or mass of any description, command it to go into the light, until there is nothing there. Do the same with the front and back, until the white room is completely empty.

Once you have done this, call down the light and ask it to go through the top of your head to the bottom of your body. Then expand your energy ten centimeters from your body, take your energy field out to the size of the room, out to the world, the universe, and outer dimensions.

When you have done this, know that you are one with everything in the universe and ask for all your soul energy that has been taken from you to be returned. When you have done this, pull your energy back close to your body and feel your awareness in your heart.

Now gently wrap yourself in a beautiful cocoon of white, purple, then silver light, following with pure gold that surrounds your whole body.

Close down your chakras, as if closing down little lights and open your eyes, as you come back gently into the room. If feeling really bad, try an Epsom salt bath.

Shelly

Shelly was a young student of mine who was a sensitive or what others may call a psychic. When she came and asked me if she could sit in my class and became a student, all I could think was how ungrounded and unfocused she appeared; it was as if she had her head in the clouds, as she was constantly vague. It was no wonder she kept complaining she could not concentrate at work. She also said she had worked in another group before, which did not suit her because she soon began to suffer from psychic attack from other petty students who were jealous of her gifts. Soon she became what she described as over sensitive and depressed. When I asked her to show me what her routine was and what she was taught when opening up to the energies in the spirit world, I saw, to my utter amazement, that she never closed down her energy properly when she was finished working or after doing any work in meditation and healing. When I asked why she never used protection or closed herself down properly, she looked at me confused and said her teacher had never told her this. This really surprised me as one of the first things I was ever taught as a student and spiritualist was to protect myself always as my own energy is sacred, and the more grounded you are the higher you can go to other levels in the spirit world. I also closed down after working or doing any type of spiritual procedure. It was no wonder the poor girl always wanted to stay home and never wanted to go anywhere and meet other people because she never had the energy. Shelly was a real-life vacuum cleaner or doormat for other people's problems, negativity, harsh energy and entities and parasites that may have been attracted to her light. When I explained to her the fundamental practice of protection, grounding her energies and closing down she said she was so grateful. She was now able to work better and efficiently, have a good life and learn more about her abilities as an eternal soul following her spiritual purpose.

Closing Down Exercise

Always remember to close down, with any type of meditation or spiritual work, exercise, or trance. Once you open yourself up, you always have to remember to close down or you will feel ungrounded and find it difficult to focus.

Now start your exercise by imagining yourself opening up all your energy or chakras, like little lights.

Once you have done this, imagine bringing down the white light, which is unconditional love, and let it enter your crown chakra allowing the light to expand all around you, outside and inside your body. Now expand this energy out to the room, outside to the city, even further to the country and now out to the universe and outer dimensions and imagining you are one with everything around you.

Now bring your energy back into the room and call back any energy that may have been taken from you by others during the day, or while out in the world.

When you are finished, always thank spirit for working with you and gently imagine all your energy chakras closing down, like little lights.

Once you have done this, visualise the white light of protection wrapping around your whole body and once again feel yourself being gently anchored to the ground, and down to the earthstar, which is situated, deep into mother earth.

The Magic of Prayer

I have always believed people who use prayer always lead successful lives. From an early age I have always believed in a higher source and this has helped me not only in my personal life, but with the work I do as a professional energy worker and medium today: my intention is to spread love on the planet and work at my highest vibration. My gift was given to me from birth and it is something I have learned to live with and take responsibility for by sitting with teachers for years in development circles. These days my teachers are my loving spirit team that are always with me by my side. Prayer is the simple magic that connects us to the source of energy and love in our world. Just as we receive love from that energy, we can receive guidance from that energy, too. Prayer is a way to put out positive energy with hopeful, healing, loving thoughts. The Christ Consciousness energy or what some may call *the universe* is the source of positive energy, the origin of love and all things hopeful and positive. It is Great Spirit's loving energy that inspires us to return that love and share it with others less fortunate than ourselves. Dark energy or negative thinking is soul destroying and the source of fear, hate and all things negative. When you send negative energy out it comes back to you tenfold, so it is important to watch your thoughts. Prayer is our way to connect to God's positive energy and to feel part of something much bigger than just ourselves. You can use prayer anytime for protection and healing not only for yourselves but also for others and you will always feel the waves of compassion and love as gentle waves of pure love and light. The gift of prayer is truly remarkable. If you are having problems in your life, that are too hard to bear, light a candle and surrender all your fears to spirit. Don't be surprised if you receive a miracle.

A Small Prayer

"Angels of love and protection, I ask for love, healing, abundance and assistance, for myself and everyone I know in my daily life, that may be suffering. I ask to always work from my highest potential and to work for service to help mankind. I also ask for healing and compassion for all the animals, birds and wild life in the world, the waterways and our beloved planet, which makes our lives divine. With love and gratitude, thank you."

Some can be cleared very easily, while others take longer, depending on what you find. If you don't want to work by yourself, you can always have an assistant that is trained, especially if it is a big job and you know several spirits are there, as it takes a lot of energy.

When attempting to work with any type of spirit, the golden rule to know is that you must always use protection at all times and be fully grounded and focused.

Ways to Ground and Center Yourself

Once you have protected yourself you need to focus and ground your energies. The easiest way to ground yourself is to breathe deeply, in and out until you feel yourself more aware and back in your body. Never work under the influence of any substance or if you are unwell and low in energy as this work takes a lot of energy and sometimes time.

Before you start to work for the day, take off your shoes and allow your bare feet to touch the earth, rubbing them in the dirt or sand. It's also very relaxing to hug a tree as you can feel the strength run through your whole body. Also rolling in the grass feels really good as well as you will feel very connected to the earth; this will dispel any negative fear-based thoughts you may be experiencing. Swimming is another way to cleanse and clear your energy as it opens up all the senses.

Rub your hands together to open up your hand chakras or energy centers and place them on your head or heart. This will open up natural, universal prana that we all channel subconsciously through our crown chakra at the top of our head.

Carry a grounding crystal like smoky quartz or black obsidian in your pocket when traveling to sacred places.

Listen, acknowledge and be aware of everything around you: sounds, smells, sights, and feelings.

Carry a bottle of rescue remedy, Bach flowers are good or Australian rescue and take four drops repeatedly until you feel better.

If experiencing cold, wrap a blanket around you, treating it like a protective comfort, as if keeping you out of harm's way.

Drink lots of water.

Eat something, as this will work instantly, even if it feels hard to chew in the beginning.

Some people claim smoking a cigarette brings you back into your body very quickly.

Crystals for Protection

I have always been big fan of using crystals for protection and abundance and love to carry a few in my pocket or bag or wear them as rings when working. In my early days I worked in healing and reading rooms all around the city where they sold many types of crystals. It was always interesting to see people coming in to stand and interact with the crystals like small children in a candy store. Once a week, one of the workers from the shop would give some of them a good soak. It was incredible really because I could literally hear the crystals sing, with my psychic ear, then they would all come out and be so shiny and bright.

Each time I worked, I would pick a crystal, clear it, and play with it for the day just to see how they worked for me. It always feels good when I can feel them in my pocket or wear them as rings or around my neck when I have important events or have to do public speaking or spirit shows. I always have them around my home as well as I love their subtle energies and have been a big collector for years.

Here are some of my favorite crystals I use with the rescue work.

Moonstone

This stone supports inner growth and strength. It also channels hope, sensitivity and abundance by wearing it. It is associated with the crown chakra and divine feminine energy and helps with intuition and psychic abilities. This looks quite pearly in appearance. Don't run this crystal under water; place it in the sun or under the moon.

Howlite

This beautiful crystal reduces tension and helps to make you feel safe and secure. It is a calming stone, and it helps the stress levels when doing spirit rescue. It also stops anger and negative energy being directed. It is able to absorb negative energy and promotes relaxation.

Blue Calcite

This crystal always soothes nerves, anxiety and stress. It is perfect for soothing and relaxing the emotional body. It not only calms emotions but offers mental and etheric protection. This is great for the aura, as it offers strong transmutational energies. I like to wear blue calcite when reading for clients and have found it very beneficial over the years.

Black Obsidian

This crystal is great for children and helps to remove blockages and fear. My daughter who is a schoolteacher always carries one when working at different schools because it helps to draw out mental stress and tension. I always carry mine when working with toxic people and clearing houses. It is made out of fast cooling lava and represents the elements of earth, water, and fire. That is why it is so powerful. It forms a natural shield against negativity, stops psychic attacks and absorbs toxic energies that have been in an environment for a long time. This is my go-to protective stone when going to big jobs.

Clear Quartz

This powerful crystal clears energies to make way for the new. It has the ability to amplify our personal energies and help us become more confident and powerful to achieve our outcomes. It is the only crystal that can be programmed. It clarifies our moods and our emotions. It can aid the steely determination of our thoughts and our feelings of psychical well-being. This stone is probably the most popular and well-known healing stone. It works as an amplifier, and you can program it to do with what you want. I use it in healing when I want extra help and carry it with me when doing rescue work. For example, I may program it to be a shield of energy to protect me when working or I can also program it for abundance or attracting angelic energies for extra help. Crystals are great to work with and programming them is a good way to start. Programming a crystal is like using affirmations, as it stores vibrations, thoughts and visions to create a positive feedback system. This means the crystal, when programmed, stimulates our whole being, rather than just our conscious mind, toward our desired goal or outcome.

How to Program Your Quartz Crystal
Clear your quartz crystal under running water or smoke with sage to remove any old or toxic energies.

Once you have prepared it, hold it firmly in your left hand, with the tip pointing upwards and ask it clearly to work with you and to give you access to its unlimited and amplifying powers. Gradually you will feel a tingling in your arm or a very subtle warm stream of energy running up your arm, depending on your own sensitivity. If you don't feel anything don't worry, it still works.

Now hold it in your right hand, same method, point facing upwards and with a clear image or picture of your goal or desire with the best outcome possible: project these thoughts or commands from your third eye and your heart, like a beam of light into the crystal. For example, "I now ask for crystalline protection, positive energy, and angelic assistance while working with my rescue work. May all my senses work in alliances with my highest good so I work at my highest potential."

The crystal is now programmed until you change it again by clearing the crystal as above. For manifestation, you need to program it again.

You can change the program in the crystal any time you want for something new when you are clearing the crystal. Quartz crystals are very good to program for abundance as well and can be placed on an altar in your office, worn on the body, or placed on a large amethyst crystal while not in use.

It is said that in one cataclysmic night, the gods from mythical times sent a battalion of fire and earthquakes so intense that the Utopian kingdom of Atlantis sank deep into the ocean, never to be found again. In my past-life meditations, I saw ancient quartz crystals in Atlantis that had magical healing properties and generated a lot of heat. People would lie on great slabs for healing and operations by the high priest, priestesses, and workers in the temples. I have also used quartz healing singing bowls, which are tuned in to our chakras for clearing energy centers with amazing results.

How to Cleanse Your Crystals

It is essential to cleanse your crystals. I like to cleanse them after each job. I spray them with salt water, place them under running water, and then set them in a bath with lavender oil. When there is a full moon, I place them outside so that they get a great recharge. Once you have cleansed them, you can start to use them again as they will be recharged.

Another way to cleanse and remove negative energy from your crystals is to cleanse them with smoke. While the smoke is flowing over your crystals, ask them clearly to assist you for their intended purpose. For example, if you are cleansing and removing negativity from an amethyst, while the smoke from the sage is around it, ask the amethyst to help you feel stress free, peaceful and content.

Energy is everywhere around us, transmitting from person to person, so it's very easy to be overcome by negative energy. Cleansing yourself, your home and your crystals regularly will help you feel more balanced, at peace and able to achieve the things you want to do in your life, such as your goals, friendships and dreams.

CHAPTER 6
CLEARING NEGATIVE ENERGY

Many of you will know the feeling associated with having negative energy in your life. If your environment feels heavy, and you feel overwhelmed, or stuck, you probably have negative energy in your life in some way which needs removing. While it might sound difficult, there are actually very easy ways to remove negative energy from your life to ensure you are able to move forward and start kicking goals again. Using sage, which is considered a sacred plant in some cultures, is one of the easiest and fastest ways to restore balance to your home.

Sage will also help remove negative energy from your body and can be used to cleanse your crystals. You can get negative energy from a buildup of toxic energy caused by arguments, domestic violence, abusive relationships, terrible neighbors, bad family members, or from others who may bring it in, often subconsciously. Often it can be left over by ex- tenants or toxic people that have been in your space. It is also good to use sage if you do any type of healing work, as often energy is left behind. You will recognize it right away as it affects everyone in some way or another including pets.

There is nothing worse than living in a space that has this debilitating energy. Over long periods of time, you will feel unmotivated, sad, confused, lonely and isolated as its toxic energy will swallow any light, love and happiness, you once had in your life. No matter how sensitive you are it will have an effect and you will emotionally, spiritually, psychically and mentally suffer in some way or manner. Often people will feel this energy immediately and find it intolerable, hampering their efforts to thrive and aim to do something about it, by complaining to others or asking what to do.

Always remember our home is the foundation to help us be successful and to have a happy life. A harmonious home creates and attracts good energy in our life.

When clearing a negative space, follow this simple method:

First, begin by clearing clutter in the space and get rid of things that take up space. Clutter stops the natural flow of energy. As consumers we accumulate far too many things over time. We will always have or collect excessive stuff that we don't need in our life. This means furniture, clothes, shoes, makeup, old cooking utensils, the list goes on. Now that you have cleared your physical space you can begin to sage.

Sage, preferably loose, is one of the easiest and fastest ways to restore balance to your home. Sage will also help remove negative energy from your body and can be used to cleanse your crystals. It can be found in alternative or new age shops and is wonderful to keep when needed in your utility cupboard. When I'm about to do a clearing, I place it in a pot with a lid, lined with aluminium foil in the bottom. When I light it and it starts to burn, place the lid on it to stop the fire, so it smolders. When I am ready, I make sure the windows are closed.

Always begin to remove negative energy from your home at the front door. Light a sage stick, then blow it out, leaving the smoke to smolder from the glowing embers on the end. Walk through the house in a clockwise direction, swirling the sage smoke as you go.

Negative energy tends to accumulate in the corners of rooms and in cupboards, so ensure you go to the corner of each room letting the sage smoke fill the area.

As you go, be sure to open all cupboards so the sage can get in there and remove all areas of negative energy.

Once you have completed the cleansing of your home, be sure to put out the sage smudge stick by placing the burning end into sand.

To cleanse yourself and remove negative energy light the sage stick in the same way mentioned previously. Holding the sage near your heart, ensure you have a clear intention in your mind that you wish to remove negative energy from yourself. Slowly pass the sage over your head letting the smoke surround your back then bring it back over your head and swirl it around the front of your body.

Once complete, put out the sage smudge stick in the same way described previously.

To cleanse and remove negative energy from your crystals, light a sage stick as described previously, then let the smoke cover them. While the smoke is flowing over your crystals ask them clearly to assist you for their intended purpose. For example, if you are cleansing and removing negativity from an amethyst, while the smoke from the sage is around it, ask the amethyst to help you feel peaceful and content.

Energy is everywhere around us, transmitting from person to person, so it's very easy to be overcome by negative energy. Cleansing yourself, your home and your crystals regularly will help you feel more balanced, at peace and able to achieve your goals.

Clearing Unwanted Spirits in the Home

Most earthbound spirits that have actually lived on the premises are hard to cross because of the attachment to the space or home. It is often common for them to think they still live there, and they are not impressed when strangers are living in their home. For people living in the house or premise, it is very frustrating when they can't get rid of the spirit themselves. However, not everyone can do this work—they may not have the right spirit team or guides that assist in the process.

In my experimental seances I run with my sitters, which is a happy mixture of mediums, healers and now good friends, they will always ask for assistance when needed. This is because, when clearing spirits, some will play games, do not want to cross and are what I call tricksters that not only hide, but continually disappear into places or outside, thinking they are safe only to reappear again once the medium has gone. I have become very aware of this and have no problems hunting them down, making sure I check everywhere.

A client told me once, every time she sage smoked her house, sometimes several times, she could hear footsteps walking outside. Things would go well for a while, then the spirit would return to continue harassing people in the home, especially her children who seemed to be getting the brunt of it all. It's amazing how children are the first to tell you about their experiences, the dark shadows walking past, the ghost that visits them in the night, or the horrible invisible thing that lives under the bed. Frustrated, she finally gave up and asked me to come, as she was so tired of trying all the time and she was at her wits end. Once I located the aggressive male spirit that kept hissing at me to leave "his" house, I was able to get rid of him very fast with the help of my spirit team. This was a great relief to everyone. It was no wonder the woman was having problems as she told me over a cup of tea that the previous owner was an evil man who was charged with child sexual abuse. When he was sent to jail, the house was sold and to her horror, ended up with the problem of his unwanted spirit once he died—he had returned back to his home, causing nothing but havoc and disturbances. One can only imagine why he did not want to cross as he was probably aware of the sins he had committed while on earth.

In my experience, once the house has been cleared of all spirits the medium should not have to come back as once the unwelcomed spirit has been crossed, it cannot return. I always reassure my clients to ring me if they are still worried or not happy as some people have terrible experiences and it takes them ages to get over it. In rare cases, I may have to clear one I may have missed, as it may have been hiding as they do, so I will do this remotely over the phone without further charge.

Another time I was called back to a house as the spirit had returned. Confused, I did not understand what had happened, as I had never had a case like that before. When I spoke to the husband, I nearly fell over backward when he told me his wife felt sorry for the female spirit, had come to like her, so as soon as I had left, called her back. The lost spirit woman who had previously lived in the house must have been very sick before she died, as the couple kept finding half eaten pills on the floor which did not belong to them. The man's wife, feeling sorry for the poor spirit encouraged her to remain in the house. Once I explained to the spirit that she could not stay and she did not belong in our world, we all joined arms together and asked her very gently to go where she could get her healing. It was a strange case and it was a good reminder for me to be more mindful of what I say: I had told the man's wife that the poor spirit woman in question was probably very lonely before she died.

For clients wanting to try and clear the spirits themselves, I always suggest to sage, but if this does not work, always ring a medium who does the work. In the meantime, I tell them to imagine in their mind's eye white light wrapping around them like a beautiful healing bubble, as this will protect them from spirits and negative or harmful energy that may come their way until the spirit is crossed. I also recommend keeping a light on, especially for children at night-time, as this slows down the problematic spirit before it is cleared. I have also found holy water to be a waste of time: although it sounds good, in reality it does nothing to help clear unwanted spirit guests. Also, I have given up wearing a talisman, which is supposed to have magic powers, or crucifixes around my neck, as I have only had them ripped off by the angry spirit.

How to Perform a Spirit Rescue

Once I have arrived and located the spirit or spirits, I will talk to it and tell it that it's dead, to open its eyes and leave because it does not belong here. I always start from the front door then make my way through each room, looking in cupboards, under beds and places spirits can hide. I generally like to go everywhere, even outside, in the garage and in the ceiling, as spirits often hide. Then, once I have located a spirit, I will visualise a porthole of white light coming down from the ceiling of the room and tell it to leave. After the spirit crosses, the energy in the room will suddenly shift to a lighter energy and balance and harmony will be restored. I keep doing this until I have scanned every section of the space, including garage, under the house, cars and attics or ceiling rooms.

After I have finished, I will make sure all the windows in the home are closed, turn off fire alarms, then give their home a good smoke out with some dried gum leaves and sage, which I burn in an old tin with some tin foil lined on the bottom. I always use a lid to stop the sage from burning with hot fire and it will suffocate the flames, causing thick smoke, which is what I want for the effect. Sometimes the place is so smoky it is difficult to see so once I have smoked every room, I will wait outside for a while, then go inside and open all windows to release the smoke. Sometimes depending on circumstances, like if the place was really toxic, I will not hesitate to do this twice to allow the clearing to go to a deeper level, making sure everything leaves. Once I have smoked each room out, it will disperse any negative energy and help any lost souls or spirits move on that may have been hiding.

After opening up windows and doors and allowing the smoke to leave it really feels like all the old bad stuff is leaving and you can feel the new energy coming in with the fresh air. Everything always looks clear after the smoke is let out, allowing everyone to feel the different energy in the home—one which becomes a lot lighter, brighter, and clearer, almost as if the heavy dark drudgery is gone. The client will also have more clarity in their life, any problems or delays will disappear and you will experience a great healing on so many levels. Life will once again become a new reality.

Once I feel satisfied with what I have done, I light a candle and slowly walk around the space, room by room, and talk to the home telling it that it is now a new beginning. I finally give it a blessing, which is always a good thing to do for the client (and the house).

Methods to Clear Energies

Always trust your gut feelings, as they are always right. If something doesn't feel right, listen to the warnings, as they are never wrong, and do something about it straight away. Never second-guess yourself and go around asking people what they think. It is your experience, and you will know what is right. Take action straight away. Here are a few common sense tips on what to do.

Smoke Cleansing

The best way to clear any unwanted energy is to do a smoke cleansing of your space. Sage may be purchased from Indigenous people, over the internet, or at an alternative shop. In my country we have many of these places and sage or smudging material is easily bought. Smudging is a sacred act to Indigenous people all over the world. There are many types of herbs you can use for smoke cleansing such as white sage, Sarimoire sage, California white sage, cedar, and palo santo sticks to name a few, mixed with other herbs, like lavender, rosemary, mugwort, juniper, frankincense, and sandalwood. You can also buy and order kits on the internet, especially made for smoke cleansing and clearing spaces. In my own experience, sage is always the best and does a wonderful job; it's no wonder I constantly use it and never tire of its strong smell that often lingers for days. In Australia, we also can use dried gum leaves, which we mix with the dried sage. Some other mediums that do the work like to place salt all around the home on the floor and around the doorways, as they say it stops spirits coming into the home, but I have found this has not worked for me.

Practical Guide on How to Clear a Space

When ready to work, place the dried and loose sage into a pot with a lid.

If you are working with a stick, make sure you break it up, making it loose and easy to burn, as it is more effective and easier to work with. Waving around a stick, will not do much as you will not have a big flame and lots of smoke.

Make a mental note to close all your windows, doors and switch off the fire alarm while doing this exercise.

When you are ready to go, light the sage. Once you have plenty of flames, blow the fire out and put the lid of the pot on. This will automatically give you very thick smoke. Remember to carry the lid with you always as sometimes you may have big flames if the sage lights up again.

Start from the front door, as this is most effective when working with lost spirits. The spirit team working with the medium will gather the lost souls up at this point in the space.

Make your way around (wearing a protective mask so as not to breathe in the heavy smoke) room by room, smoking everything in sight, opening cupboards and checking under beds. Don't forget to do the attic, basement, garage, outside buildings, cars, and roof area if you can get into it, as these are common places spirits can hide. Spirits like to move around, through doors, walls and never stay in the same area. I like to do this a couple of times to make sure I have covered every area.

Once you have done this, the smoke will weaken the spirit, which will subsequently go or move on, as the sage will repel and weaken the spirit. I walk around the house outside with sage in case the unwanted spirit has stepped out and is hiding, waiting for the whole procedure to finish, only to come back in again when I am gone. If you live in a flat or apartment and the spirit escapes through the walls, I recommend to sage the place once a week to make them not want to visit.

After waiting for at least twenty minutes, open up all windows and doors allowing the thick smoke to clear. As it leaves, you will see how "clean" and good your space will feel.

If you are still having problems call in a medium or someone who does the work with rescue. If you have problems looking for the right person—and yes there are a few that cannot do the work, even though they say they can—I always suggest to people to contact their local spiritual church as they are generally highly sympathetic and know mediums who do the work in their congregation, or outside that are reliable and honest for a reasonable fund.

Don't ask for the help from unscrupulous types that are only out to con you, asking for high fees and continually wanting to come on a weekly basis, or even make threats.

Land Clearing and Indigenous Lost Spirits

This work is best done by an Aboriginal or Indigenous elder or asking someone that is Indigenous to assist. Unfortunately, if I cannot find the right person I will step up and become involved in land clearings where there have been lost Indigenous spirits that once lived on the land. I begin this by first protecting myself, with any work I do, saying a prayer and calling out to the spirit elder of the tribe for assistance. As working on clearing land, this is easy to do, because as an empath you can feel with all your senses the "psychic trail" of what went on and where the lost spirits are, just like you are working in a home or large space. I love to do this work, as I love nature and have a great respect for the Indigenous people as they have a deep spiritual connection to the land and the surrounding nature. Our history tells us with all countries in the world with Indigenous cultures, of the cruelty of our colonial past, and we have all heard and read of events where our Indigenous people were killed, murdered or treated badly on their land and sacred sites. Sadly, it makes sense that there would be lost souls among this category of spirits who have not crossed and are still lost and wandering.

Sue and Greg

A lovely couple called me one day to an isolated property where there was nothing but ongoing problems in the home and surrounding land. Things were constantly going wrong for no reason and they were at their wits end, as even their animals were dying and all their machinery was breaking down. Crying on the phone, the distressed woman said the once happy family were non-stop fighting since the day they moved in. She was convinced in her bones, something bad had happened there and she had no idea what it was. The constant bad energy that lingered everywhere and the unexplainable feeling of grief she felt was indescribable and starting to wear her down. She kept saying the home and the land was perhaps cursed or haunted, as she was constantly surrounded by weird shadows, that flashed by her eyes and the land and trees all around her felt sad as if they were grieving. It was no wonder the family had constant nightmares whenever they had the opportunity to sleep.

When Sue finally spoke to her neighbors, she was told, to her dismay, the original owners had struggled for years with weird things going on all the time. The problem went back in history to when the original white owners fought with the custodial Aboriginal leader who claimed the land was his. When the Indigenous man died, there was nothing but bad luck and trouble for most people in the whole area: it was indeed, as if the land was cursed.

On my arrival I quickly protected myself, and after I began to walk around and around, blessing the land and smoking the land with dried gum leaves, my spirit guide, White Feather, told me to go out to the back of the house to the fence. Once I reached there, the overgrown space was full of thick weeds that seemed to choke some of the trees. As I pulled the weeds away, Sue and I saw an old plaque of an Indigenous man's face hidden under some thick roots. Tuning into my guide, I heard a voice tell me that the woman and family, if they wanted to live in peace, were to honor the land, respect its guardianship from the Aboriginal people and to place a bowl of water, as an offering under the man's face. I then told the spirit that this would be done and asked him to collect his people and leave. When I told Sue, she said this simple act would be done and as the new owners of the property she would make an offering every day to respect the elder and the tribe that once lived there. My only assumption was the bad luck, negative energy ,or curse would be released, and it was time for healing and for people to move on. I also told Sue to smoke her home with dried leaves if she was to ever have any problems. A couple of months later, she rang me and said the family could not be better and she had no use for any gum leaves.

Alex

This story will be about an experience I had with a Jillinya, a spirit woman or mermaid in Australian Aboriginal culture. Years ago, while on a fishing expedition in the Kimberlys with my husband, I could feel and sensed a female spirit watching me as we slept in a tent. As I tried to open my eyes, I could not move my body, and

I felt my spirit guide push me in the middle of my back and lift me up out of the bed into a sitting position. I saw a very beautiful woman spirit with dark skin, a round face, big eyes and long black matted hair that hung down to her shoulders. It was like looking at a ghost that had come out of the sea.

When I described this to our guide, an Indigenous man called Alex, he laughed and said I had witnessed a Jillinya spirit. According to folklore, Alex explained that if you want a wife, you can grab her if you are fast, but you have to be clever. Because she is in spirit form, you need to take a knife and cut beneath her feet very quickly as she is floating next to you. I'm told this will cut the cord that connects her to something, Ibut it was unclear what she is attached to. You will then see blood dripping on the ground. This is when she is manifesting from spirit form into physical form. You have to grab her and tie her up and whip and beat her and flog her until she starts to cry and howl, and you will see tears coming from her eyes. She is then yours to be your wife. You have to teach her to talk and do all the things that you want her to do but you must not let her go near the river or any rock pools because if she sees her reflection in the water, she will vanish back to the sea. You have to keep her away until she forgets where she is from.

Why she came to me I will never know, and I can only think she may have been tracking our guide, Alex. The next day I saw her depicted on rock art sites all around the north Kimberley coastline.

Uluru

Uluru or Ayers Rock is called the "Island Mountain," and has a distinctive red coloration at dusk. It is an amazing and powerful place where I have had different experiences each time I have visited it. Today it is listed as a World Heritage site and belongs to the local

Indigenous people called the Anangu. Every time I visit sacred sites, I feel full of so much energy where as others may feel tired and have naps all the time.

The local people take great pride in this amazing sacred space and are the custodial owners of the land. When I visited the site, I could see a dark, ominous face looking at me, which seemed to be carved in one of the rocks. Shivering with fright, I understood the energy of the place was sacred and the spirit of the rock did not want me there. Understanding this, I excused myself and told the rock I was sorry and asked for forgiveness for my ignorance, all the while wrapping protection around me. Since that time, the custodians of the land have stopped people climbing the rock because of its great spiritual significance to them. Climbing of the rock ceased permanently in October 2019. It is a place that has a high energy and many believe that like most sacred places, those who take rocks will be cursed and forever suffer misfortune. Uluru and the country around it affected me energetically because I found it impossible to sleep. I also witness many spirit orbs, all different and just floating around, quite easy to see with the naked eyes.

Being an open vortex of energy, it was full of what I can only describe as high voltage energy, which seemed to flow and pulse in little waves throughout my entire body from my head to my toes. It was like an energy circuit going around my body. A vortex is best described as a whirlwind of moving matter in the shape of a spiral (sometimes described as tornadoes) that can be suppressed, plugged and stopped. The earth has many vortexes in many sacred spaces like Sedona and Uluru where ley lines or energy lines cross. It is said natural vortexes can provide us to travel energetically between dimensions, so it's no wonder you may feel like you are going out of your body, feel sleepy or the other end of the spectrum—feel energized. They tend to exist where there are strong concentrations of gravitational anomalies. A portal, on the other hand, is an entry point, bridge, doorway or gateway between two locations, or dimensions. They can be a conduit for dark and negative energies and entities. Once opened they can be a conduit for new and positive light frequencies. We can open and close them to get rid of negative energies or entities that don't belong in this dimension. We aim to open portals to evolutionary energies and close them to the dark areas of the astral plane.

REMOTE VIEWING
AND CLEARING

Remote viewing is the practice of seeking impressions about a distant or unseen target, purportedly sensing with the mind. Not only is it safe and very practical but very effective, especially in times of great stress and worry. It does work—I use it all the time and it is easy to learn. Remote viewing is very similar to telepathy and the remote viewer is expected to give information about an object, event or person that is hidden from physical view. It is also described as the practice of seeing impressions through the third eye a great distance away and works with extra sensory perception or what is more commonly known as ESP. With a bit of practice, the remote viewer can give information about an object, or even a person in any location. After learning the process and feeling confident, I began to use it to check on my elderly parents who live a great distance from my home, so I did not have to worry. I still use the phone, but the technique helped me get stronger when working this way.

When I was working on a late-night television show and people were phoning me from all over the country asking me to clear their homes of unwanted spirits and negative energies, I found remote viewing to be helpful. Initially when I signed up for this job, I thought I would just be doing mental mediumship or answering psychic questions. It was uncanny that I was to clear energies over the phone remotely, which is known as spirit rescue. This was highly successful. It didn't seem to stop there because the need grew bigger, and I now clear energies and do spirit rescue over the phone on a daily basis with great success. It's easy to do, saves time and travel, and always works. I truly believe that if Spirit wants you to work in a special way, it will give you all types of gifts so long as you don't misuse them and your intention is pure in helping people. Psychic people, empaths, healers, and mediums will find that if they misuse their gifts or harm anyone in any way for their own benefits, they will often lose their gifts.

Remote Clearing

Whenever a client wants me to do a remote healing and clearing of lost spirits or negative energy, I make a time and date with them and my spirit team, similar to a contract. Once this is affirmed, I ring them as arranged.

Once I make initial contact, I explain to them what to do. The first thing is to put me on loudspeaker. Then I ask them to imagine a white light of protection wrapping around them and to go to the front door—the mouth of the house or property where we will begin the clearing. We will walk together through every room, including the garage, roof, and basement, to scan the property. I also explain I will do any buildings in the yard or connected to the property.

I like to start from the front door, the mouth of the house, for a reason. This is because my team of spirit helpers are already there, and it is very common to find a lost spirit there, as if it has been pushed to the front of the home. It is amusing how this always works, because every time, without fail, the spirit team knows exactly where to go and what to do.

Once located, I can describe if the lost soul is male, female, or, in some cases, an animal, and what they look like. I am also able to know if they are earthbound, if they lived in the home or are the home's previous owner, and what type of spirit they are. The earthbound spirit that has lived in the house is difficult to remove as they often still think the home is theirs and don't understand why people are living there on their property. It is no wonder they are quite determined not to go and can cause havoc, especially when it comes to renovations, or people wanting to make changes. It is quite common to find wandering spirits hanging around as well. They are different from the earthbound, are generally very confused and I often find these types in clusters, gathered around together. These are easy to get rid of as they often do not have any type of attachment to the home: you just need to give them a sage out if a medium cannot come and cross them.

When I have explained to the client what is going on, I ask them to imagine or visualise a portal of white light coming from the ceiling and to say these words out loud:

"Go into the light, go into the Holy Spirit, open your eyes and leave. You are dead and don't belong here. Go. Go now. Leave, you are not welcome and need to cross. Your loved ones are waiting, don't be afraid, leave now."

This is repeated several times or until I feel the spirit is moving and crossing.

Once this is done, the client will feel some type of shift, hot or cold air, or the space will feel suddenly warmer. They also will commonly experience goose bumps, with all their hairs standing up on the body. They usually let you know the space feels better and are happy and relieved to say so. You may also see little dots or light energy floating around and the vortex that was opened to send the spirit off will always close after the spirit leaves.

Gradually we move from room to room, repeating the previous steps, opening up large cupboards, where a spirit could hide or looking under beds and sending any lost souls off, until I am satisfied that we have nothing left.

When the session is over, I always ask the client if there is anything left that makes them feel uncomfortable.

Development Exercise to Practice Remote Viewing

This is an easy to learn exercise and I have taught this many times to my sitters, in my seances and also with students over the years with my trance and mediumship. With practice, anyone overtime can learn how to do it. You don't have to be psychic just be patient and open up your mind. It teaches us just how unique we really are, when we understand how energy works. Once you learn how to do it, you will no longer have to worry about loved ones when you are not there.

Once, when doing the exercise with a student who was not understanding the exercise, the student accidently went to her grandparents' house and met her maternal grandfather and other relatives she had never met, as they had died many years before. It was as if she went backward in time. Overwhelmed with happiness, she could not stop crying and said it was the first time she had met them. She explained that her grandfather and older cousin had died when she was young. When we discussed this in the group, I explained she had gone back on her timeline, through her love and her family, which was very healing for her. It was one of those moments in your life you never forget and demonstrates the power of our minds.

Meditation

Find a sacred space in your home, by the sea or a beautiful place in nature where you will not be disturbed.

As you close your eyes, slowly breathe gently in and out; in through your nose and out through your mouth, until you feel centered and grounded.

With your intention place a beautiful light of protection all around you, including under your body like a protective bubble of white, pure light. The white light is a powerful source and can protect you always against anything.

Now as you gently breathe in and out expanding your energy and consciousness, push your energy out five centimeters from your body, then increase the expansion so that your energy is the size of the town, then to that of the country, now the world, and finally out to the universe.

Once you have done this, bring your energy back again slowly, understanding that you are one with everything around you.

Now, I want you to think of somewhere you want to travel. For example, if it's at your family home, imagine yourself standing at the front of the house. As you stand there, you look at the garden, the fence and anything that comes up or you remember. It may be emotions, smells, how it made you feel and what it looked or looks like.

Once you have done this, take yourself to the front door, counting the stairs if any, but before you enter the home, ask for permission to go in to visit the occupants. Once you get *yes* in your mind, which is from their higher selves, slowly go through each room, noting what the occupants are doing and if they are safe in their environment.

When you feel confident that all is well, close the front door behind you and wrap white light around the home. After you feel confident, open your eyes and know your family is safe.

If practiced, you can really expand on this and will be even able to see what they ate for dinner and where they are in the house the time you did the remote viewing. To get confirmation, perhaps phone them and mention anything you saw. You will be surprised with what you get and the positive feedback, which in turn, will give you the confidence to keep working in this way.

This is an example of how I helped a woman remotely over the phone.

What Is That Smell?

Years ago, I was doing a radio show and my interviewer Garry had several people ring up to ask me psychic questions. A number of them wanted proof of survival after death. We had only just finished the first few calls when a rather nervous woman came on the line and started telling me about a disturbing and weird smell that kept following her around everywhere. I immediately sensed that we were dealing with a spirit who probably just wanted to get a message across.

The poor woman sounded quite embarrassed when she revealed that the awful smell that had been following her relentlessly for months was a strong male body odor and that it was quite offensive. The situation sounded quite funny the way she described it, but I could sense her fear was indeed very real and no laughing matter. I quickly reassured her that nothing bad was going to happen because she started to softly cry over the line and must have been quite stressed. I am glad I followed my instincts and listened to my guide's advice, because as soon as I said this the poor woman let out a huge sigh of relief, laughed nervously and went on to tell me the rest of the story.

She described a strong male "boofy testosterone smell" that not only lurked around her at home when she was alone, but also followed her to work. It seemed to turn up everywhere she went, even arriving at places before she got there. This really scared her as she travelled all over the countryside with her work and no matter where she stayed the smell was always there. Over time she began to loathe the stench as it reminded her of her dreadful ex-husband, whom she hated and despised. He was still alive but she had nothing to do with him after their terrible divorce years before. The smell now was starting to negatively affect her and she was beginning to think she was going mad or having a nervous breakdown.

Shelley went on to tell us that she had a very responsible job, was high up in her company and was terrified to tell anyone, let alone her workmates, in case they thought she was crazy. The poor woman was now starting to think that perhaps the smell must have been some type of payback or bad energy from her nasty ex-husband, who had been cruel to her when they were married. It had taken years of soul searching and a lot of courage before she had the strength to finally leave, but she was now convinced that he must have paid someone to curse her to make her life miserable. I sensed this was utter nonsense and told her so straight away. I also felt the husband was probably not aware of what was going on.

I gently reassured her that she was going to be fine and that she was definitely not crazy. I then went on to tell her very gently that this smelly phenomenon was called clairalience or clairolfaction, which means psychic smelling. It is a type of psychic phenomenon in the same way as rapping (things that go bang in the night) and mysterious visions of spirit people or ghosts that sometimes show themselves to unsuspecting people for no apparent reason. When I told her this, it definitely lightened the situation and we all cracked up and had a good hearty laugh over the airways.

Within a few seconds, spirit started giving me messages for Shelley. These began to come through very quickly and the so-called smell was a male relative of the woman's ex-partner trying to bring through a message of love. When I told Shelley this, she shuddered and confessed the smell did remind her of her ex-husband and she recalled his father also had a similar odor when he was alive.

The spirit said his name was Ray and, as soon as I said this, Shelley started crying and said this was indeed her former father-in-law. She said that she had been quite close to him while he was alive. The spirit man had been dead for many years now and since his death Shelley had separated from her husband and they were no longer on talking terms. Once Shelley realized what the smell was and that it was not going to hurt her in any way, shape or form, she began to relax and seemed relieved. The spirit man went on to say that her ex-husband could not move on because of his hatred for her. Not wanting to get involved, I sat and waited to see what she had to say.

"Too bad. That is his problem," she hissed bitterly, annoyed and not wanting to listen anymore. "I cannot stand the man and I no longer want anything to do with him. He can rot in his own hell for all I care."

After I rang her privately about a week later and removed the unwanted spirit remotely over the phone, Shelley got in contact with me again. She seemed happier and laughed over the phone. This time she rang to thank me for all the help I had given her with her terrible problem she had been going through. As far as she was concerned everything was now back to normal as she wrote a for-giveness letter like I suggested to herself and forgave her nasty ex. Once she did this, she was confident that the awful smell would never come back and haunt her ever again.

Someone once told me it was not good to have more than one string to your bow, but I sincerely believe that is not true, as spirit will never stop teaching you things and you will never stop learn-ing until your spirit contract on earth is over.

The Troublesome Home

One day I did a phone reading and remote clearing in my office for a client called Annie, who lived in America, and had endless prob-lems with her health, work and frequent arguments over menial things with her partner. No sooner had I connected to her voice, which is always a psychic link, than I told her she had a grand-mother around her in spirit who had once lived in a small town in the country. The spirit woman went on to tell me she had died of a heart attack and was breathless before she passed. She also said she loved Annie, who was an only child, and had been a gentle girl who loved riding horses when she was younger.

When I told Annie this, she laughed, delighted to hear from her grandmother and said she wasn't surprised, as they had always had a special connection when she was alive. She had always looked forward to the delicious cream buns her grandmother bought her when she was younger. As I went further into the reading, I sensed Annie's whole life was now totally exhausting and was not surprised she was ringing me for guidance. According to the grandmother, Annie's young daughter was very unsettled as well, suffering from anxiety attacks and fearful—too afraid to sleep in her room during the night. Intuitively I knew she had a problem of a spooky nature—I could sense the paranormal activity in the home as we talked. From my own experience as a psychic child, most children are very open and naturally psychic. We should never ignore a child or judge them when they tell us things, as often it is not stories from their incredible imaginations. Tuning in, it did not take me long to see that there were what I first sensed— lost spirits in the home that were causing Annie and the family problems. When I asked her if all the problems started happening when she moved into the old home she bought with her partner two years before, she paused and said yes. She then continued to tell me that the couple who previously owned the home ended up getting divorced and she had heard they had to sell as they were at logger heads and fighting for a long time in a court case. Looking back on her life, she realized it was a struggle since they moved into the house and her initial feeling of not wanting to buy it was correct. This confirmation was clarified almost instantly, because as soon as I closed my eyes I sensed and saw a vision with pictures in my mind's eye of some type of muddy unsettled gray energy lingering in the home, which indicated to me the house without a doubt, was haunted and causing endless imbalance for the inhabitants. Making a time with her, I managed to clear the home over the phone and found three spirits lingering in different areas of the home. The house must have been over a hundred years old: I saw a spirit woman sitting on a chair on the front veranda dressed in old-fashioned attire, wearing some type of bonnet. I found an older man in the kitchen cupboard and finally a younger man, quite youthful in appearance upstairs in a bedroom. All three spirits seemed confused, so I knew they were earthbound and were sent off very easily into the light to the spirit world.

Each time Annie walked into different parts of the home with her phone on loudspeaker, I could feel the energy very strongly. A couple of months after the clearing and reading over the phone Annie rang me and informed me that things had settled in the home, and like my prediction, the sale of the house went ahead without a hitch. They were no longer having problems and had also put a deposit on a new home. She was relieved and excited that she no longer felt sick and couldn't wait to move on to their new home and journey. As for Annie's small daughter, once I removed the spirits from the old home, things started to improve for her as well and I was over the moon to hear she was no longer feeling anxious all the time.

Distance or Remote Healing

Distance or remote healing through the use of intention is a valuable tool in which healing and love can be sent anywhere in the world. It is a non-invasive practice, as it holds the intention of restoring things back into harmony and balance. This positive, coherent energy can calm down any situation and take away a lot of stress and worry quite rapidly. It is good to use when you are worried about a loved one, and it can help diffuse a toxic situation where there is imbalance in the home, property, or space.

Love is the greatest force you can use your intention for. Energy can be sent via thought and emotion and can be completed over any distance, small or vast. Not only is it easy, but it's also free and does not take a lot of time. Everyone will benefit from this and feel improvement in themselves, and the once-fractured energy of the space, home, or land. Remember distance healing can be used on anything.

Many years ago, in my development years, I studied spiritual healing, which is the transfer of energy through the healer to a recipient from the spiritual churches and later Reiki healing. Reiki is a form of alternative therapy, using symbols that can be done hands-on and over great distances. I later realized this type of healing was a valuable tool to use in every single aspect with my work as an energy healer. Not only do I send distant healing to loved ones, clients and people I know, I also send healing to places in the world, the environment and places that are suffering from imbalances and pain—all with good results.

After the Australian bush fires that caused total havoc in many states and soon after the devasting floods, I sent out healing to the people, animals, birds and land. It broke my heart to know that over a million koalas were burned to death along with their habitat, and that there were so many deaths with people losing their homes. It gave me a great feeling of relief sending out the healing daily, and I am sure it helped in the healing process for everyone involved. These days I also work to distant healing to send to homes or places that have a lost spirit causing problems before I get there to calm the spirit down. When I do home visits and remote rescue work, I always send healing afterward. This helps to increase the healing and help restore any imbalance to the clients, due to lack of sleep, trauma caused by the unwanted spirits, negative thought forms, depression due to stress and negative feelings and emotional blockages. A number of clients will say that they feel like they have been in a war zone and were mentally, psychically, and spiritually exhausted. Negative energy does affect you and, with this type of healing sent, will help in the healing process.

Remote and distant healing is easy to learn and a valuable tool to know and to use in our daily lives. Everything works through intentions and if everyone used it, we would feel empowered and have more peace in the world.

How to Do Remote and Distant Healing
Find a sacred space in your home, by the sea or a beautiful place in nature where you will not be disturbed.

As you close your eyes, slowly breathe gently in and out; in through your nose and out through your mouth, until you feel relaxed, centered and grounded.

With your intention, place a beautiful light of protection all around you, including under your body, like a protective bubble of pure white light. This is your protection. The white light is a powerful source and can protect you against anything when used, as it is pure love.

Now as you gently breathe in and out expanding your energy and consciousness, push your energy gently out five centimeters from your body, then increase the expansion so that your energy is the size of the town, then to that of the country, now the world, and finally expanding it out to the universe. Once you have done this, slowly bring your energy back in.

Now in your mind's eye, imagine a big pink healing bubble of love. Once you have done this, place this bubble around the family one at a time and ask their higher selves if they would like some healing. Once they have said yes, ask the higher powers that be to send love and healing. I always call on help from the angelic kingdom when I do this. Once you have opened up your energies and surrendered to the higher powers, with your eyes closed, using the palms of your hands, direct streams of purified energy into and through the aura or through the sufferer in order to disperse congestion in the etheric and emotional bodies and to drive out harmful substances. This will restore the harmonious and rhythmic flow of the client's life forces, which are out of alignment due to illness. It may take time if the client has been sick for a long time. Once you have done this, invoke in the higher energies by calling out in your mind's eye the healing angels and the Christ energy and leave the rest to the invisible forces of the angels and the higher powers for the healing.

If you want to do individual healings, spirit will always assist you and show you where the illness is in the body. I always suggest after the absent healing to use white sheets, as spirit and the healing angels can continue while you sleep.

Other Absent Healing Methods

Another way of sending absent healing is to write on a piece of paper the names of the people, place, or home that you want to send healing to. Place this paper under a white candle and light it.

You can also use a picture of the home, family, pets, or people involved and send healing energy this way. It is always necessary though to close your eyes and ask their higher selves for permission first before you do anything and place them in the pink bubble. I love to use Mother Mary in my healings as she is a wonderful energetic energy for miracles and is loved by millions.

CHAPTER 8
ASSISTANCE FROM ANGELS AND SPIRIT GUIDES

Archangels are the highest rank of angels anyone can work with as they appear in the religious texts of Gnosticism. I always imagined angels as magnificent beings without bodies. They are highly empathic, intelligent, kind, and are messengers of God, which we often see in churches in pictures, with halos or light around their heads. I also imagine them with great wings as I have seen this in apparitions and meditations, and they have been described like this from clients and friends. Angels are messengers from the spirit world and highly intelligent. Their one mission is to help and assist us mere mortals. They are harbingers of beauty and kindness and offer assistance in anything that we need, especially healing in any shape or form. They are also known as God's children. We also learn about them in religion, such as Judaism, Christianity and Islam. Throughout the ages, angels have been portrayed as having human form, performing certain tasks, then disappearing quickly again. In my experience, they often take human form and can look like anyone or anything. With spirit rescue, I work with not only my own spirit team, but with chosen angels all the time. This makes me feel more confident as one never knows what will happen on any day. Each type of entity is always different. Sometimes, when talking to the earthbound spirit, you may have a situation where the confused spirit will become stubborn and may not go—it will try to hide or disappear outside the space that is being cleansed until I leave. To make sure this does not happen and I will not have to be called back by the client, I ask these six archangels—Michael, Gabriel, Raphael, Uriel, Azrael, Chamuel—to help and assist me on the day.

To invoke their help and assistance, I just call out their names for assistance on the day and thank them afterward. I have also heard of stories of angel intervention and it's wonderful to know these do exist.

Archangel Michael

Michael is the "bouncer boy" of the Archangels from the higher powers that be. No matter what the challenge is or what you are going through, all you have to do is ask him for his help, as he is always ready to protect and serve humanity in any way. This divine energy will clear the way, give you strength and courage and will always be there for you in the dark and rough times of your spiritual rescue work. The first time I saw this angel in trance and meditation I was completely overwhelmed. It was a very big energy and I asked if he could assist me with my work. I sense this magnificent being as a strong warrior energy who carries a shield and a sword—you know when he is around. Call on him for extra protection when dealing with hauntings.

Whenever I am feeling rundown, under psychic attack, need to cut cords with toxic life lessons, or just need help in any situation, I light a candle, say a prayer and call him in. Within minutes of doing this, I feel a strong protective loving force of pure energy by my side, and I know I don't have to worry anymore. Whenever you have any problems in your life, call out to Archangel Michael and know that things will be miraculously resolved.

Archangel Gabriel

The Archangel Gabriel is the bringer of good news and hope. This angel is related to the element of water and is related to the sacral chakra, which is connected to deep trauma, shock and past memory recall. When I first met this energy in meditation and trance, I visualised the energy as being feminine because it was so nurturing and gentle. I saw a beautiful woman energy, with soft fair hair, large gentle eyes and pleasant in appearance. I call this energy my special magic to help me manifest or help remove whatever I may need in the physical world.

When you call on this energy you will receive wisdom and love required to evolve to a higher good. In my experience, Gabriel ensures us victory with anything we ask for, especially creative projects. This angel fills us with inspiration, confidence and positive energy, so no matter how hard the task is, you will always have a positive outcome, especially with new jobs. This is a good archangel to use when running any type of groups, as it inspires the group energy to work together as one and let go of any perceived failures and insecurities. Sometimes I would feel scared going to haunted houses and wondered indeed if I would be okay. I should never have doubted myself because time has shown me with my spirit team and the angles to assist nothing bad ever happens when you pray for help and have the faith.

Archangel Raphael

This is the angel of healing and protection as his name means "God heals." The energy of Archangel Raphael governs the solar plexus with the element of air and rules our subconscious thoughts. The name meaning implies we can shift our consciousness and heal ourselves if we believe.

When we call in this energy, we call in all that is hidden (known as your intuition); it brings great clarity into your life. When I first channeled this energy, I saw the energy as a combination of male and female and when I asked my students, they all had different views except for the healing aspect, which was exceptional. I visualised a powerful entity dressed in a green gown with long brown hair. All over the world this angel is also known as the patron of healers and those in need of healing. It is believed that this mighty Archangel is able to fearlessly move into whatever area is needed in healing, bringing a host of Angels with him to accomplish this.

I affectionately call this energy *my miracle angel* because any problems you may be having, such as health, money or relationships, this energy will clear the obstacle in most cases. Invoking this angel also brings peace to others and he is often used by light workers, counselors and anyone who works with energy and the power of love and light. When traveling through southern Europe, my husband and I saw this patron saint almost everywhere we went, not only in churches but also in the architecture in many of the buildings and surroundings.

This sighting of Archangel Raphael all around me in my travels, was not only a big greeting, as I adore this angelic being, but a personal signpost that I was safe. It reinforced that I would be watched over and for me to enjoy myself as I was in alignment with my inner faith, ideologies and beliefs.

Archangel Uriel

This angel means light of god, bringing divine light and healing to painful burdens from the past into our lives. This energy has the element of earth and is red in color. It focuses on expectations and psychical restrictions and allows the light of wisdom to shine on your subconscious mind. When I met this angel in meditation and trance, I saw it as a gentle being. In addition to the color red, I also saw sine orange and yellow, reminding me of the beginning of autumn. I call this angel the Archangel of forgiveness, as its energy helps release anger, resentment and past memories that can be responsible for mental pain and illness. There is nothing more toxic than negative thoughts and emotions in our body and cells. It has been proven time and time again that these thoughts can lead to disease. The reason I use this angel is to help lost spirits move on.

Archangel Azrael

Archangel Azrael's name means "God helps," and is known as the angel of death and transition. This powerful archangel helps with the transitional time the soul is ready to leave the planet and join up with loved ones and soul groups in the spirit world. As this is an adjustment time, he is able to help the spirit and the loved ones left behind, filling us with hope and wisdom and assisting us in the vital grief period. Archangel Azrael helps ministers, mediums, carers and spiritual teachers from all belief systems and religions in their spiritual counseling. When called upon, he will help you shield from absorbing the pain and grief that is part of this process. This archangel assists in all types of transitions and endings, not just those involving loss and death.

Azrael helps with transitions related to relationships, career, addictions, etc., helping us to navigate as smoothly as possible through life's changes. When we go through great change, no matter what it is, we can call on our loved ones from the spirit world and this great powerful angel for assistance and we will receive guidance, great love, healing, comfort, compassion, and inspiration to guide us step-by-step as Archangel Azrael acts as a bridge from our world to the afterlife. He also sits on the panel in the spirit world for the life review at the end of our life. Archangel Azrael can be called upon while you are still alive to help you assimilate the many lessons that you have learned in your current existence; he can help with past and future lives, enabling you to raise your energy to access the Akashic Records.

Archangel Chamuel

Archangel Chamuel means "He who seeks God." He offers us his gift of Peace, welcomes change, and allows love and balance to come into our lives. His energy is powerful, magnificent, pure, and the holiest flame of divine universal love that exists in the spiritual. He is one of seven archangels living in God's presence in Heaven. He can be called on to help with relationship issues, as he brings great clarity and inner healing to the situation, helping opponents come to an agreement. He's very helpful with politicians, leaders, or people with authority because of his calming and inner drive for better, calmer outcomes and realities.

As you work with his energy over time you will feel consumed with unconditional love and an inner understanding and knowing of peace. You will have a better understanding of what is going on and you will be able to read energy better. As you forgive and have compassion with your situation and open yourself to self-love, your vibration will rise and you will release all fear, no longer attracting negative or toxic destructive relationships in your life and at times repeat themselves as in the Law of Attraction.

The Archangels Meditation

This is a good meditation to know that these angels are here to assist you in any area of your life. They are here to serve mankind and love to do so. It is good to know they can be relied on when you call them into your circle of spiritual friendship in times of great change and need you may be going through. It is a wonderful feeling when you evoke them so you can use them with you with sometimes difficult work. The Archangels will give you the assistance that you need when you simply call out to them.

Find yourself a quiet space and breathe deeply three times, till you feel yourself relaxing.

Now in your mind's eye, visualise the colors of the energy chakras: red, orange, yellow, green, blue, indigo, and violet.

Once you have done this, imagine yourself sitting on a tropical beach, with pristine white sands as far as the eye can see, a blue sky and calm waves in the background, gently breaking on the sand. It is a peaceful place and nobody is there except you and nature.

Now in your mind's eye, focus all your intention on what you want and let all the problems of the day go.

First, call upon the Archangel Michael. Ask him to present himself to you. As you do so, let go of any fear and distrust in your higher self. Let go of any negative emotions that may block your spiritual sight. Feel his loving energy as he stands next to you.

Call on the Archangel Gabriel so that you receive wisdom, abundance and love required to evolve to a higher good. Feel the loving energy as this angel stands next to you. This is the angel of victory.

Next is Archangel Raphael, for all that is hidden is now known as my intuition. Feel the healing energy of this amazing angelic energy. Say, "I now have clarity of vision. I feel the healing and loving energy coming to assist me."

Archangel Uriel is next. Allow light and wisdom to shine down on you.

Feel the love as this great angel stands next to you.

Call on the Archangel Azrael, to help with the transmutation and transition of any old beliefs and worn-out concepts you may be harboring with your spiritual work and journey.

Now finally call on the healing archangel Chamuel the healing angel of love, peace and change. Feel the powerful love of this great angel, surround you and wrap you in great wings.

Once you have done this, ask them for assistance in any area of your life you may need help with. You can call on them all together or separately, whenever needed. Understand by invoking them and acknowledging their heavenly existence, you can call on their assistance when needed, as angels are always ready to assist us in any capacity where needed to help mankind.

When you have finished, thank the angels, close down by closing all your energy centers, as if they were little lights and then sweep white light through you. When you have done this and you feel fully connected to the earth and your body, give gratitude.

My Spirit Rescue Team

I am very blessed, through dedication to my work, to have a very good collection of loving, highly evolved guides in my spirit team. They are an integral part of my life and without them I could not do this work. To this day, they always give loving assistance with mediumship, my private seances and my healing work, which includes past-life regression. I have been a practicing medium for many years and did a lot of training in my early development days in spiritual churches and groups, as I had no understanding of what was going on and what my spiritual gifts were. You too with practice, patience and dedication can learn to work with your own guides as well. It reminds me of the old saying "When the student is ready to learn, the teacher will always appear." These days I continually learn a lot of information from my own experiences and different cases, as not all are the same. I am constantly given assistance and have communication with these spirit helpers when needed. It works exactly like the communion of Angels, that are here to assist us on earth. They will only form a presence and step in when you pray or ask them for assistance. They will not intervene unless you ask for their divine help. Once you receive the help, you always thank them. When I need my spirit helpers I call on them, as I know they are always present, as we have a working contract so they stay in the background, while I have my own life's experiences for my own spiritual growth. When I have finished my work I thank them and know they are always at my side in times of difficulty or work.

When I do spirit rescue work, the other guides step aside and these move forward to assist in the process. Through regular meditation and trance, you too can meet your guides to assist you not only in your daily work but any type of paranormal or spiritual work you do. You will find the more you work with spirit rescue, the more help you will always receive through spirit. Nothing is never too hard or too difficult, as it seems they know what you are capable of, as spirit always looks after you. These days before I go to a place or do remote viewing the spirit team is already there, ready to help with assistance. Their job is to round the lost souls up at the entrance of the home or pull them out from their hiding places, making it easier for me to rescue them and cross them over. Without their loving assistance I would never be able to work between two worlds, other realities and other dimensions. I like to know as much about them as possible as it gives me the extra confidence that I am always being assisted by my heavenly helpers.

White Feather

White Feather is my main guide or *gatekeeper*. I have seen him in meditation and trance as a huge Indian chief with a big head dress and has been with me from the beginning of my spiritual journey and work. In mediumship, our gatekeeper, or main guide is usually a highly evolved spirit guide we have had a past life with, or made a connection with in the spirit world that is extremely loving and caring. The rapport we build up and the contracts we make with our gatekeeper help protect our aura and chakras from unnecessary and inappropriate energies when we are consciously doing the work of a light worker or energy worker. Our gatekeeper stays with us always and protects our soul until we pass over to spirit world, receive our life review and join our soul groups once again, before we journey back to earth or other worlds, through reincarnation. In some circumstances, guides will occasionally go and work with other healers, psychics, energy workers and mediums. We are multi-dimensional beings and well-known guides can be present in many dimensions and places at once. I found this out first hand when some of my students told me that a few of my guides visited them in the sleep state or in a meditation. At first I had no idea this could happen but found overtime, I also have worked with other guides, belonging to other people. They never stay but they do lend themselves out for the healing and learning process.

When I first met White Feather in a meditation, I heard a gentle voice talking to me in my ear. The gentle male voice introduced himself and told me that he was my main guide and had been with me since birth and would assist with my own transition when my time was finished on earth. He said his name was White Feather or Father.

Gradually I began to channel him more clearly and picking up a pen and a piece of paper, I began to draw him, a beautiful old man with deep kind eyes with a full headset of beautiful feathers on his head. He explained that we had been in a past life together, he had been the chief of a great tribe and that I had been his only son. That made sense to me as I love nature and often dream of riding horses as a young American Indian man, next to a rushing river. I have also had many past lives of living in a simple place, with lush grass and huge mountains somewhere in America, long ago where I have been women and men in different lives. Some of these lifetimes were wonderful and horrific because of the lessons and learning of the soul. White Feather said he was looking after me with my mediumship, and not to be afraid as he would guide, assist and protect me always. He told me that the work I would be doing was important for many people. Often when I am called out for work, I will always find a white feather sticking up in the ground, which is a signpost to me, loving spirit is always looking out for me and no job is ever too hard.

Dr. Lee

Dr Lee is a healing Reiki guide who first appeared when I studied and became a Reiki master in my early years. He works with energy and meridians within the body. He is quite serious, dedicated and very bossy. He is a small Oriental gentleman with tiny little hands who wears his hair in a long plait. He has a restless nature, similar to my own, and is a curious intelligent being who likes to get on with the job at hand. When I began working with his energy, I was attracting numerous clients who may have had cancer, or other serious problems with their body. I found I also started doing psychic surgery with my healings. I had no idea what I was doing, but just surrendered to the energy and acted as a pure channel for the work that needed to be done. Spiritual psychic surgery is a non-invasive event to the physical body and operates by drawing negative energy out of the energy body or field, removing deep-rooted blocks of stagnant and negative energy out the body and energy centers or chakras. It also removes thought forms and memory implants or what we call *soul retrieval*. If not removed, these energies can create disease leading to strangulation of the organs and body parts on an emotional and physical level as it blocks the life force and can lead to long-term health problems. This type of hands-on healing is completely different to the psychic surgery that is practiced in the Philippines and other areas in the world where tumours and other diseased tissue is actually removed from inside the body. Reiki energy and other methods of spiritual healing works successfully with all types of conventional healing and can accelerate the healing process. I would never suggest to a client to go off their medication unless their doctor told them to do so. I also learned to do many good crystal layouts using crystals as grids and laying the stones on the body's energy centers. The more I did this work, the more the clients came. It was if I was in training with my spirit guide, and I ended up spending years perfecting this ability. As soon as I developed myself further and became attuned as a Reiki Master and Seichim Master, Dr. Lee came straight into my energy field and I began to do a lot of psychic operations on clients. Dr. Lee was very forthright and wanted to get me doing psychic surgery more and more as the phone never stopped ringing with clients wanting to book. I was shown and taught so many things about the human body through this wonderful guide. I found I could sense things about people and their diseases and was encouraged to learn more at different courses and schools. I found that as soon as I sat down and closed my eyes, healing energy would be channeled from this guide. Having studied spiritual healing, and being a qualified Reiki master as well, I basically already knew the fundamentals. I still channel this wise guide's wisdom and use his energy in other ways, and he always helps with the rescue work, especially when clearing land as I use the healing symbols.

Margaret

Wise Margaret is an older female guide or crone who once worked as a clairvoyant and healer in England. She said she was branded a witch—this was because of the time on the planet she worked on. When I connect to her energy through trance, she speaks with a distinct English accent and tolerates no nonsense. She works with flower essences, mediumship and rescue work. She has also taught me how to remove entities from the aura, how to do spirit rescue and how to get rid of spells and curses. Margaret lived in the 18th century and did not like the church as it condemned her type of work, even though all she ever did was help people to heal or reach their loved ones on the other side. I have had the most amazing insights by working with this very kind and humble guide as she is constantly teaching me things I could not possibly know or even have read in a book. With my guide Margaret and her assistance, I am also able to remove what we call entities, which are lower vibrational parasites from the aura, the energy around the human body. We sometimes pick up these energies when the outer layer of our aura becomes thin and breaks or rips. This can happen through drug use, shock, long-term sickness, trauma, alcoholism, accidents, and stress and so on. Once I have scanned an aura with my hands and third eye, I am able to send these pests into the light for healing. I am also able to remove curses that may have been around for centuries and can be very harmful for people. Most people know when they have a curse on them, which is just negative energy, as nothing works in their lives, no matter how hard they try, and they go around and around, never getting anywhere. Luckily for them, once they are onto it, they will find someone who can help them and who works in this department. Their loving spirit guides will guide them to a reputable healer who does this work. I always feel safe when Margaret is around; she is very competent, no nonsense and knows exactly what she is doing.

Red Hawk

Red Hawk is a gentle energy and guide who works with my rescue work, by helping in the transition process of crossing lost souls over to the spirit world when I command them to go into the light. He looks like a young American Indian with long dark hair and wears simple clothes. He stays very much in the background, saying little, but is happy to give assistance when needed. He is very humble, and I feel I have been a brother to him in a past life as an American Indian. Every time I channel him in trance, I feel like I am also riding a horse bareback on a great open prairie. He always comes with great messages of reassurance that in death we are never alone in our journey to the other side.

How to Meet Your Own Guides

If you are wanting to build up your own spirit team, or spirit helpers, this is easy to do and, if practiced with patience and love on a regular basis, will help you connect to your own loving guide who is always with you from birth until death. When the energy builds up, new guides will come in all the time and want to work with you, but when you are working on different things some step back when they are not used. Your main guide, or gatekeeper, stays with you all the time and never leaves—they are your faithful companion till death. For example, if are working with spirit rescue, you will have a team, with other guides stepping in.

Meet the Guide Meditation

Find a quiet place where you will not be disturbed. Sit in a comfortable position and breathe deeply until you feel your whole body relaxing, gradually slowly releasing as you exhale any tension from the day and any negative thoughts, emotions or mindset you may imagined falsely in your mind, creating unnecessary fear, which is misinformation.

Now imagine a protective bubble of pure white light, wrapping around you or a white pyramid filled with the golden holy light of protection and love. The white light is a powerful force and can protect against anything in the world.

As you do this, imagine your mind being like a brand-new blackboard and you are now dusting it off creating a clean space, full of fresh ideas, hopes and inspirations.

Visualise energy in the form of white light coming down from the top of your head and moving slowly down through the chakras to your heart center, filling your whole body with love. Feel this energy and, with your own aura, expand it as far as you can take it.

Now bring it back and take it down to the rest of your body and center it deep into the earth below you.

In your mind's eye, slowly count to ten, and then imagine you are in the grounds of a beautiful garden. In your mind's eye, look around you and imagine all the details—hear the breeze sighing through the trees, smell the wafting fragrance of beautiful blooms, feel the soft green grass under your feet, and see the blue sky above.

Feel yourself relaxing more and more, as you visualise what your garden looks like. Once you have created your inner garden of peace and tranquility, call in your own loving guide from the light and feel the presence of eternal love.

Once you feel a presence, ask your guide if it is from the light. If it says no, send if off to the light and continue asking your guide to step forward until you feel you have connected to your true guide from the light.

When you have connected, ask for healing or any information you may need to help you on your journey. Take your time and fill your soul with gratitude, as you are now able to connect with your soul's energy and your inner power. When you are finished, come back in to the room and imagine the golden triangle being placed around your own energy field.

Once you are back in your body, gently close all your energy centers down by flushing them with white light. Always remember to close down all your chakras or energy centers.

Don't forget to offer gratitude to spirit for everything you have in your life, and remember your guides are here to work with you anytime you like; you just have to call them in and ask for assistance.

CONCLUSION

Through my many years of rescue work and experience, as a working medium, I am convinced that there are a large number of lost souls on the planet that need this valuable work. They need help as they do not belong here.

The difference between living spirits, (spirits that have crossed) and earthbound or lost souls, (spirits that have not progressed soul-wise to the next level because they are stuck) is they are so easy to talk to and will often go to great lengths to get a message of love across. They also know everything in our life and once you are connected, you know that help of a spiritual nature is always there offering assistance through signs, such as dreams, songs, feathers, perfume, coins, to name a few. So, when going through difficult times, you can often feel the spirit of a loved one very close by.

Living spirits offer healing and love, watch over us always and hear all our prayers. I don't know how many times a client has rang me up and not known why. Before too long I am able to hear a spirit voice coming through with messages of love and information the client needs to know. This is called spirit intervention and is remarkable when it occurs.

Lost and earthbound souls are very different as they are confused, sometimes aggressive, stubborn and difficult to talk to. This is because they are stuck in the astral, which is a miserable, bleak, and cold dimension. It is as if they are walking on the earth plane upside down.

Hauntings and stories of paranormal experiences and different types of phenomena have been witnessed and experienced for as long as time itself. Throughout the history of mankind, we have always had paranormal incidents and ghostly encounters with an eerie and unexplainable nature to say the least.

All of my stories are true and not something I have just heard or made up. I have experienced them firsthand but just the names are different. The thing is all these stories can happen to anyone and are real. Once you understand how it all works, help is at hand.

Throughout history, whenever we have some type of unexplainable occurrence of a spooky nature in our home, place of work or community, the holy man, seer, wise woman, medium, or healer is called on to assist in any way they can or at least give us some type of explanation of the goings on in our environment that tends to cause so much fear, anxiety and confusion.

Always seek assistance if you have any type of problem and please do not be afraid; the lost soul is only trying to get your attention and needs help and assistance so it can be passed over. Understand what you are dealing with and yes, there is always somebody to help and assist you. Everyone deserves to have peace, love and healing in their life. If you do not know a medium who is experienced in spirit rescue, contact your local spiritualist church.

Never be afraid to ask for help, there is always somebody to listen and believe you with lots of answers for all your questions.

Blessings, love, and light.

RECOMMENDED READING

Barbanell, Maurice, and Silver Birch. *They Shall be Comforted*. London: Spiritual Truth Books, 1938.

Cannon, Dolores. *Between Death and Life*. Huntsville, AR: Ozark Mountain Publishing, 2013.

———. *Convoluted Universe*. Huntsville, AR: Ozark Mountain Publishing, 2001.

———. *Nostradamus*. Huntsville, AR: Ozark Mountain Publishing, 2013.

Chase, Pamela, and Jonathan Pawlik. *Healing with Gemstones*. Newburyport, MA: New Page Books, 2001.

Erwin, Kerrie. *Clearing*. Wirral, UK: Rockpool Publishing, 2019.

———. *Mediumship*. Wirral, UK: Rockpool Publishing, 2020.

———. *Sacred Signs*. Sydney: Love and Write Publishing, 2016.

———. *Sacred Soul*. Sydney: Love and Write Publishing, 2015.

———. *Sacred Space*. Sydney: Love and Write Publishing, 2015.

Newton, Michael. *Destiny of Souls*. Woodbury, MN: Llewellyn, 2009.

———. *Memories of the Afterlife*. Woodbury, MN: Llewellyn, 2007.

Stein, Diane. *Essential Reiki*. New York: Penguin, 1995.

Webster, Richard. *Dowsing for Beginners*. St. Paul, MN: Llewellyn, 1996.

To Write to the Author

If you wish to contact the author or would like more information about this book, please write to the author in care of Llewellyn Worldwide Ltd. and we will forward your request. Both the author and the publisher appreciate hearing from you and learning of your enjoyment of this book and how it has helped you. Llewellyn Worldwide Ltd. cannot guarantee that every letter written to the author can be answered, but all will be forwarded. Please write to:

Kerrie Erwin
℅ Llewellyn Worldwide
2143 Wooddale Drive
Woodbury, MN 55125-2989

Please enclose a self-addressed stamped envelope for reply,
or $1.00 to cover costs. If outside the U.S.A., enclose
an international postal reply coupon.

Many of Llewellyn's authors have websites with additional information and resources. For more information, please visit our website at http://www.llewellyn.com.